STECK-VAUGHN
Spelling

John R. Pescosolido, Ph.D.
Professor Emeritus
Central Connecticut State University
New Britain, Connecticut

Consultants

Felice M. Rockoff
Reading Teacher
New York City Public Schools
New York, New York

Theodore J. Thibodeau
Assistant Superintendent
Attleboro Public Schools
Attleboro, Massachusetts

Anna L. Ulrich
Adjunct Professor
College of Santa Fe
Albuquerque, New Mexico

Anita Uphaus
Coordinator of Early Childhood Programs
Austin Independent School District
Austin, Texas

STECK-VAUGHN®
COMPANY
ELEMENTARY • SECONDARY • ADULT • LIBRARY

Acknowledgments

Executive Editor: Diane Sharpe
Project Editor: Amanda Johnson
Design Manager: Richard Balsam
Designers: Jim Cauthron
           Danielle Szabo

Product Development: Cottage Communications
Typesetting: Publishers' Design and Production Services, Inc.

Writers: Bonnie Brook (pp. 30, 38, 44, 56, 88, 94, 108, 114, 126, 134, 140, 167, 178); Linda Ekblad (p. 70); Bobbi Katz (pp. 172, 173); Stuart Podhaizer (Etymologies); Les Purificación (p. 102); Linda Rogers (p. 120); Maxine Schurr (p. 146); Lorraine Sotiriou (p. 18); Judith Bauer Stamper (pp. 6, 12, 24, 50, 62, 76, 82, 113, 127, 152, 158, 166, 184, 190)

Artists: Bob Barner, Maxie Chambliss, Betsy Day, Julie Durrell, Allan Eitzen, Jon Friedman, Jon Goodell, Carol Grosvenor, Konrad Hack, Meryl Henderson, Ron Himler, Ruth Hoffman, Joan Holub, Kathie Kelleher, True Kelley, Elizabeth Koda-Callan, Dora Leder, Tom Leonard, Susan Lexa, Carolyn McHenry, Linda Miyamoto, Ed Parker, Jerry Smath, Joel Snyder, Arvis Stewart, Michael Tedesco, Arthur Thompson, Joe Veno

Grateful acknowledgment is made to the following for the use of copyrighted materials. Every effort has been made to obtain permission to use previously published material. Any errors or omissions are unintentional.

Pronunciation key and diacritical marks in the Spelling Dictionary copyright © 1994 by Houghton Mifflin Company. Reprinted by permission from *THE AMERICAN HERITAGE STUDENT DICTIONARY.*

ISBN 0-8114-9273-7

Contents

Lesson 1   Words with /ă/

Listen for /ă/ as you say each word.

match

magic

ask

past

crack

snack

stamp

pass

grass

happen

answer

travel

plastic

began

banana

glad

branch

half

laugh

aunt

1. Which words end with /k/? _____

_____   _____

2. Which words end with /ch/?

_____   _____

3. Which word ends with the same three letters as <u>lamp</u>? _____

4. Which word ends with the same two letters as <u>sad</u>? _____

5. Which word ends with the same three letters as <u>last</u>? _____

6. Which word ends with the same two letters as <u>ran</u>? _____

7. Which word ends with the same five letters as <u>gravel</u>? _____

8. Write the words that contain double consonants.
ss _____   ss _____

pp _____

9. Write the word in which you see the letter <u>w</u> but don't hear /w/. _____

10. Write the word in which you see the letter <u>l</u> but don't hear /l/. _____

11. Write the word that has three syllables.

_____

12. Write the words in which /ă/ is spelled with two vowels. _____   _____

4

Checkpoint

Write a spelling word for each clue.
Then use the Checkpoint Study Plan on page 224.

1. Today I begin, yesterday I ____.

2. as yellow as a ____

3. not cry, but ____

4. A bad trick is tragic ____.

5. Eight is to four as whole is to ____.

6. Another word for question is ____.

7. not the future, but the ____

8. When you get 100% on a test, you ____.

9. Some dishes are made of ____.

10. Give a gift to a father and make a dad ____.

11. not question, but ____

12. You put this on a letter. ____

13. Body is to arm as tree is to ____.

14. A broken cup probably has a ____.

15. To take place means to ____.

16. as green as ____

17. A light meal is a ____.

18. Race is to run as tour is to ____.

19. not your uncle, but your ____

20. Homographs are words that are spelled alike but have different meanings. The mystery word is a homograph. The first meaning comes from the Old English word *macche*, meaning a husband and wife. The second meaning of the word comes from the French word *meshe*, meaning candle. Can you guess the mystery word? ____

Use each spelling word once to complete this story.

A Summer Storm

Willy followed his sister down the path from their aunt's cabin. Nilda was hurrying to the lake.

"What's taking you so long?" Nilda turned to _____ Willy.

"I am trying to catch up," was Willy's _____. He was carrying a bag of apples, a _____, and a big _____ cooler. "I just stopped to get a _____ for us to eat."

"I wish there was some _____ we could work to get to Cane's Island in a flash!" thought Nilda, looking at her watch. "It's already _____ three."

They pushed their canoe into the water. As Nilda _____ to paddle, Willy ate his apple. He looked up at the sky.

"I don't like the way the clouds look," he said.

"Oh, they'll _____," Nilda said. "Come on and help me out. I've covered _____ the distance by myself."

Willy was able to _____ the speed Nilda set. The canoe glided across the lake.

Suddenly, there was a loud _____ of thunder. The two stopped and looked up.

"We have to get off this lake!" Willy shouted. "I was afraid this might _____."

They looked around, wondering if they should _____ on or go back to the cabin.

"Back to shore," they shouted at once.

Lightning flashed across the sky and the rain began to fall.

Finally, the canoe reached the shore. Willy and Nilda made a run for their _____'s cabin. Pushing away a broken tree _____, Willy fell onto the wet, green _____. At last, they reached the cabin and rushed inside.

Willy and Nilda began to _____ their wet shoes on the cabin floor and wring their soaking clothes.

"Wow, that was close," Nilda said, looking out at the choppy waves. "I'm _____ we're off that lake!"

Willy nodded and began to _____. "I'm glad that I was there. How would you have gotten to safety without me?"

"A lot faster," Nilda smiled. "That's how!"

7

match
magic
ask
past
crack
snack
stamp
pass
grass
happen
answer
travel
plastic
began
banana
glad
branch
half
laugh
aunt

Alphabetical Order

Dictionary words are listed in alphabetical order. Words beginning with a come first, then words beginning with b, and so on. It is simple to find a word in the dictionary if you know about alphabetical order.

★ Write the words in each group in alphabetical order.

1. laugh   crack   travel

_____

_____

_____

2. plastic   magic   aunt

_____

_____

_____

★ When words begin with the same letter, look at the second letter to put the words in alphabetical order.
Write the words in each group in alphabetical order.

3. began   banana   branch

_____

_____

_____

4. aunt   answer   ask

_____

_____

_____

5. snack   stamp   squirrel

_____

_____

_____

6. glad   grass   gold

_____

_____

_____

★ If the first two letters are the same, look at the third letter. Write the words in alphabetical order.

7. half   happen   harm

_____

_____

_____

8. match   magic   map

_____

_____

_____

Challenge Yourself

acrobat   axle   absence   tragic

What do you think each underlined Challenge Word means? Check your Spelling Dictionary to see if you are right. Then write sentences showing that you understand the meaning of each Challenge Word.

1. The absence of clouds made us forget that a storm was coming.

2. The road was very bumpy. We thought the wheels on our car would fall off the axle.

3. The newspaper reported the tragic story of three people lost at sea during a storm.

4. The wind made the leaf leap and tumble like a circus acrobat.

Write to the Point

Have you ever been caught outdoors in terrible weather like Willy and Nilda? Write a brief story about what happened, or use your imagination to make up a story. Tell where you were and what the weather was like. What did you do to escape the bad weather? Use spelling words from this lesson in your story.

Challenge Use one or more of the Challenge Words in your story.

Proofreading

Use the proofreading marks to show the errors in the paragraph below. Write the five misspelled words correctly in the blanks.

Should people traval by car during a thunderstorm If you ask me, the anser no. Car accidents often hapen on slick roads. Wait the storm to pas. You'll be gladd you did.

⬭	word is misspelled
∧	word is missing
⸮∧	question mark is missing

1. _____

2. _____

3. _____

4. _____

5. _____

Lesson 2   Words with /ā/

Listen for /ā/ as you say each word.

chase

awake

mistake

trade

waste

taste

plane

space

state

shape

paid

plain

afraid

trail

wait

waist

eight

weight

neighbor

break

1. Which words end with /n/? _____

_____

2. Which words end with /d/? _____

_____

3. Which word ends with /k/ and has one syllable? _____

4. Which words end with /k/ and have two syllables? _____

_____

5. Which words begin with the letter w? _____

_____

6. Which word begins like train and ends with the same three letters as pail? _____

7. Which word begins like toy and ends with the same four letters as paste? _____

8. Which word begins like check and ends with the same three letters as case? _____

9. Which words have the same spelling of /ā/ as freight? _____

_____

10. Solve these: sp + ace = _____

sh + ape = _____

st + ate = _____

11. Which words begin with the letter a but have the schwa sound /ə/? _____

_____

Checkpoint

Write a spelling word for each clue.
Then use the Checkpoint Study Plan on page 224.

1. Haste makes ___.

2. The opposite of asleep is ___.

3. A running track is a race ___.

4. not fancy, but ___

5. Texas is a ___.

6. Ruler is to height as scale is to ___.

7. Another word for swap is ___.

8. "Two plus two equals five" is a math ___.

9. Once in a blue moon means it's a long ___.

10. You hike through the forest along a ___.

11. You wear a belt around your ___.

12. The opposite of mend is ___.

13. A search for a suitcase is a case ___.

14. The number after seven is ___.

15. sight, sound, smell, touch, and ___

16. Filled with fear means ___.

17. Today I pay, yesterday I ___.

18. Another word for form is ___.

19. Ocean is to boat as air is to ___.

20. This mystery word comes from the Old English word *neahgebur*. *Neahgebur* is made of two separate words. They are *neah* and *gebur*. *Neah* meant nearby. *Gebur* meant farmer. So *neahgebur* meant a nearby farmer. Now the mystery word means someone who lives near someone else. Can you guess it? ___

11

A PIONEER FAMILY

An old wagon bounced along a narrow path. The Palmer family was headed toward a new

_____ and a new life. It was 1820 and they were on their way to Kentucky.

"John," his wife called. "Tell Billy to come inside the wagon."

A look of surprise came over John Palmer's sleepy face. He glanced at the empty _____ beside him. Wide _____ now, he pulled the horses to a halt.

"Billy isn't with me," he said.

Suddenly, they both knew the truth. Their

_____-year-old son was lost!

"Emma, we can't _____ time! When did you last see Billy?"

Emma answered, "The last time we stopped, he ran off to _____ some berries. I thought he got back in the wagon with you."

"I wish I had _____ more attention," John sighed.

"John, I'm _____. What are we going to do?"

John jumped down from the wagon and grabbed his rifle.

"_____ for me!" shouted Emma. "I'm coming with you."

12

Emma grabbed another gun and ran with her husband down the _____. As they looked for some sign of Billy, John and Emma came to a dead stop. Before them stood the huge _____ of a bear. He was circling a tree. From high in the tree, a voice yelled, "Ma! Pa!"

They looked up and there was Billy, the top branch of the tree barely holding his _____.

John lifted his gun to the sky and a loud shot rang out. The bear ran into the forest.

Emma walked over to the tree and helped her son down. Billy hugged his mother tightly around the _____. He sobbed, "I'm sorry, Ma."

"We all made a _____, Billy, but it's over now," John said, hugging his family to him.

"You might say that we 'barely' made it," Emma said with a smile.

"Aw, Ma!" groaned Billy.

- A bear began to _____ Billy.
- Billy thought the branch would _____.
- Pioneers used to _____ with Native Americans.
- A pioneer's closest _____ was often miles away.
- 1820: covered wagon
  1980: jet _____
- 1800's: _____ log cabins
  1900's: big, fancy homes

13

chase
awake
mistake
trade
waste
taste
plane
space
state
shape
paid
plain
afraid
trail
wait
waist
eight
weight
neighbor
break

Punctuation

A sentence that tells something ends with a period.

My favorite sport is basketball.

A sentence that asks something ends with a question mark.

What sport do you like best?

A sentence that shows strong feeling or surprise ends with an exclamation point.

My team is the best basketball team in school!

★Write the sentences below. Correct the misspelled word in each. Add the correct punctuation mark to the end of each sentence.

1. I live in the stait of New York

2. My weith is seventy pounds

3. Wate for me

4. How did you brake your leg

5. Will you traid your bike for mine

6. Are you afraid to fly in a plaine

7. The tatse of this food is terrible

8. I'm in great shaep now that I jog every day

Challenge Yourself

lightweight   betray

acquaint   reign

Use your Spelling Dictionary to answer these questions. Then write sentences showing that you understand the meaning of each Challenge Word.

1. Can you <u>acquaint</u> yourself with people by talking to them for a long time?

2. Would good citizens <u>betray</u> their country by selling its secrets to an enemy?

3. Do dark clouds often come before a <u>reign</u>?

4. In summer do most people wear <u>lightweight</u> clothing?

Write to the Point

Suppose that you and your family could move anywhere in the world. Where would you like to move? Would it be another part of your town or city? Would it be another state or country? Write a paragraph telling where you would want to move. Explain why you want to live there. Use spelling words from this lesson in your paragraph.

Challenge Use one or more of the Challenge Words in your paragraph.

Proofreading

Use the proofreading marks to show the errors in the paragraph below. Write the five misspelled words correctly in the blanks.

	word is misspelled
≡	letter should be capitalized
✐	take out word

some pioneers liked lots of space. They were not afrayed to be alone. if they payed a visit to a naighber, they often had to be be awak by dawn and travel a rugged trale.

1. _____

2. _____

3. _____

4. _____

5. _____

Lesson 3 Words with /ĕ/

Listen for /ĕ/ as you say each word.

edge

ever

never

echo

energy

fence

stretch

yesterday

desert

bread

ready

heavy

health

breakfast

weather

sweater

again

against

friend

guess

1. Which words begin with a consonant and end with a vowel? _____

_____

_____

2. Which words begin with a vowel and end with a consonant? _____

_____

3. Which words begin and end with a vowel?

_____ _____

_____

4. Write the words in which you hear /k/.

_____ _____

5. Which words end with /s/? _____

_____

6. Which words end with the letters er?

_____

_____

7. Write the word that begins with the letter d.

_____

8. Write the words that end with the letter d.

_____

9. Which word ends with the letters tch and the sound /ch/? _____

10. Which word ends with the same five letters as wealth? _____

11. In which words do you see the letter i but do not hear /ĭ/ or /ī/? _____

_____

Checkpoint

Write a spelling word for each clue.
Then use the Checkpoint Study Plan on page 224.

1. Wood is to chair as wool is to ____.

2. The opposite of sickness is ____.

3. If you're not for, you are ____.

4. The baker was poor, so he kneaded ____.

5. To be prepared is to be ____.

6. not light, but ____

7. A little rubber band is a short ____.

8. Always means ____.

9. Rock is to mountain as sand is to ____.

10. To speak before you know all is to ____.

11. Good food and exercise help give us ____.

12. When mountains talk back, it's an ____.

13. not enemy, but ____

14. Repeat means to do something ____.

15. A thick gate is a dense ____.

16. The opposite of always is ____.

17. Cup is to rim as table is to ____.

18. not today or tomorrow, but ____

19. as changeable as the ____

20. Have you ever fasted? To <u>fast</u> means to go a long time without eating. A <u>fast</u> is a time during which we have not eaten. We all fast when we sleep at night. Our first meal of the day ends, or breaks, our overnight fast. The name for this meal is our mystery word. Can you guess the word? ____

17

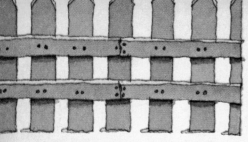

Use each word once to complete these pages.

RACKETEERS

The autumn _____ was just right for tennis. Seymour C. Skunk tied his white _____ around his shoulders. He ran to the court, feeling full of _____.

"If only I had someone to play with," Seymour sighed. "But people always turn up their noses at me. They whisper 'P-U' under their breath. Well," Seymour promised, "I will _____ try to make friends _____."

With a _____ heart, Seymour gave the ball a smack _____ the wall.

"Wow! Great form!" thought a young rabbit. So she hopped through the _____. Her clapping caught Seymour's attention.

"How about a game?" he asked.

The rabbit smiled. She followed him to the tennis court.

After the game, Seymour invited her to have some _____.

"_____ to order, sir?" asked the waiter. He was holding his nose.

"Mademoiselle will have the Forty Carrot Cake and I'll try the Spinach Surprise. And bring some French _____, please."

Seymour glanced fondly at her. "What's your name?" he asked.

The rabbit turned up her nose. She gave Seymour quite a start.

"I'm Beatrice Lapin," she answered in a soft voice. "But my friends call me Bunny."

"You know, Bunny," said Seymour slowly, "_____, my life was sad. But today, I don't think I've _____ been so happy. I _____ I never thought I'd find a _____ like you."

Bunny's nose moved again. Seymour jumped to the _____ of his seat.

"There's something I must ask you," Seymour began. "It's a rather scent-sitive subject. Don't you find that my smell bothers you?"

"Why, Seymour!" Bunny said. "I thought you bite have noticed. I have a bad code!"

- Tennis is good exercise. It is good for your _____. It helps to strengthen and _____ the muscles.

- Seymour was always alone. He felt as though he was living on a _____ island.

- When Seymour spoke, no one answered him. All he ever heard was the _____ of his own voice.

19

Guide Words

Guide words are the two words in dark type at the top of each dictionary page. Guide words make it easy to locate a word. The first guide word is the same as the first entry word on the page. The second guide word is the same as the last entry word. The other words come in between in alphabetical order. When searching for a word in a dictionary, always check the guide words first to see if a word is on a particular page.

---

closet | club

clos·et | klŏz′ĭt | *n.* **1.** A small room or cabinet for hanging clothes, storing linens or supplies, etc. **2.** A small private room for study or prayer. —*v.* To enclose in a private room, as for discussion: *He closeted himself with an adviser. They were closeted together for hours.*

close-up | klōs′ŭp′ | *n.* **1.** A picture taken at close range. **2.** A close or intimate look or view. —*modifier: a close-up picture.*

clo·sure | ~~a clothing store.~~ ing ~~klo chər~~ | *n.* A rule in a legislative ~~body~~ that cuts off debate so that a vote may be taken.

cloud | kloud | *n.* **1. a.** A visible object of fairly indefinite shape formed of a collection of water droplets or ice particles suspended in the air. **b.** Any similar object formed of suspended particles or droplets, as of dust, steam, or smoke. **2.** A moving mass of things on the ground or in the air that is so large and dense that is appears to resemble a cloud: *a cloud of locusts.* **3.** Something that depresses ~~or~~ *The bad* ~~which or sweet.~~

cloy·ing | kloi′ĭng | *adj.* Excessive to the point of being distasteful: *cloying praise* —**cloy′ing·ly** *adv.*

club | klŭb | *n.* **1.** A heavy stick, usually thicker at one end than at the other, used as a weapon. **2.** A stick designed to drive a ball in certain games, especially golf. **3. a.** A black figure, shaped like a trefoil or clover leaf, on a playing card. **b.** A card bearing this figure.

★ Look at the four pairs of guide words below. Then read the list of words under each pair. Write the words that would be on the same dictionary page as the guide words.

1. after / agree

ace _____

again _____

age _____

against _____

2. eat / eerie

elbow _____

east _____

echo _____

edge _____

3. head / height

health _____

help _____

hamster _____

heavy _____

4. straight / sweet

stamp _____

sweater _____

stretch _____

switch _____

Challenge Yourself

kennel   sheriff   cleanse   deafen

Decide which Challenge Word fits each clue. Check your Spelling Dictionary to see if you were right. Then write sentences showing that you understand the meaning of each Challenge Word.

1. You should always do this to a cut or scrape before you put on a bandage.

2. This person's job is to make sure laws are kept.

3. A very loud sound near your ear could do this to you.

4. You might say this place has gone to the dogs!

Write to the Point

Seymour C. Skunk was unhappy until he found a friend. Write a paragraph about a person who is your friend. Tell why you like having that person as a friend. You may want to tell some of the things you enjoy doing with your friend. Use spelling words from this lesson in your paragraph.

Challenge Use one or more of the Challenge Words in your paragraph.

Proofreading

Use the proofreading marks to show the errors in the paragraph below. Write the five misspelled words correctly in the blanks.

Yestarday morning I ate a good brekfast. I wanted to have lots of enrgy. My frend maria and I played tennis for two hours. the wether very hot, so I didn't need my sweater.

◯	word is misspelled
≡	letter should be capitalized
∧	word is missing

1. _____

2. _____

3. _____

4. _____

5. _____

Lesson 4 Words with /ē/

Listen for /ē/ as you say each word.

knee

queen

between

sweep

sweet

speech

seem

freeze

squeeze

scream

reason

season

treat

beach

teach

means

speak

leaf

peace

please

1. Which words end with /z/? _____

_____ _____

2. Which words end with the letters ch? _____

_____

3. Which words end with the letter t? _____

4. Which word ends with the letter n and has one syllable? _____

5. Which words end with the letter n and have two syllables? _____

_____ _____

6. Write the word in which you see the letter c but you hear /s/. _____

7. Write the word in which you see the letter k but don't hear /k/. _____

8. Which word begins with three consonants? _____

9. Which word ends with the same three letters as beak? _____

10. Which word ends with eem? _____

11. Which word ends with the same three letters as sleep? _____

12. Which word has the same first and last sound as laugh? _____

Checkpoint

Write a spelling word for each clue.
Then use the Checkpoint Study Plan on page 224.

1. A new broom is a clean ____.
2. Another word for yell is ____.
3. Saturday is to day as summer is to ____.
4. At Halloween, it's trick or ____.
5. To talk is to ____.
6. Your leg won't bend without your ____.
7. Things are not always what they ____.
8. Branches are to branch as leaves are to ____.
9. A fruity talk is a peachy ____.
10. What something is all about is what it ____.
11. Ten people in a phone booth is a tight ____.
12. Water is to ocean as sand is to ____.
13. You do things for a good ____.
14. The opposite of melt is ____.
15. After war comes ____.
16. The opposite of sour is ____.
17. not in front or in back, but in ____
18. To be polite say ____.
19. A woman ruler is a ____.

20. This mystery word is related to the Old English verb *tacnian*. *Tacnian* meant to be a token or a sign of. Later the word was changed to *techen*. *Techen* just meant to show. Our mystery word looks very much like *techen*. Now it means to instruct or to guide in education. Can you guess the word? ____.

23

Vana's Big Race

It was the day of the big race. The track team was having its last meet of the _____. The score was tied and this was the most important race. Vana stood with the other runners, waiting for the last race.

"I'm scared," she said to her friend Ellen.

"You're scared," Ellen shouted. "This morning I could hardly _____."

"Really, you always _____ so calm," Vana answered.

Coach Talbot was kneeling on one _____, giving his same old _____.

"I'll make this short and _____," he said. "The one thing I've tried to _____ you is that it's how you play the game that counts. Just because this race _____ the school championship, that's no _____ for you to be scared."

Ellen gave Vana's hand a _____ and she whispered, "I think you'd better win!"

Vana took her place at the starting line. Suddenly, she felt weak. She was afraid that she would _____ up at the starting shot.

"Starting places, _____," the judge began. "On your mark, get set . . ." Bang! The runners were on their way!

Vana was off to a slow start. She heard her friends _____, "Faster, Vana, faster!"

Vana began her kick as she rounded the last turn. Now, she was ahead of all but three runners. With only a few yards left, Vana passed in _____ two more runners. The crowd began to roar. Vana felt as though she were flying! Soon, the front runner began to drop back. She had used up all her energy in the beginning. Vana felt herself _____ past her and break the tape. The home team won!

Coach Talbot threw his arms around his team and said, "Come on, girls. You've earned a _____. I'll take you out for ice cream. And you don't have to skimp! You can each have a _____-sized cone!"

"Thanks, coach, you're a sport!" the girls teased. And they all piled into his old blue car.

1. Vana exercised every day by jogging along the _____.

2. Vana's trophy had two gold leaves and a single silver _____.

3. After the race, Vana was thankful for a little _____ and quiet.

knee
queen
between
sweep
sweet
speech
seem
freeze
squeeze
scream
reason
season
treat
beach
teach
means
speak
leaf
peace
please

25

Verbs

A verb is a word that expresses action.

I <u>ran</u> across the street.

★ Find the verb in each group of words and write it.

1. speak   peace   plain
_____

2. leaf   neat   teach
_____

3. team   scream   queen
_____

4. between   sweet   freeze
_____

5. cheese   squeeze   knee
_____

6. sweep   girl   swan
_____

★ Jessie writes the daily schedule at summer camp. Here is the schedule for July 12. Make a list of the verbs in the schedule. Also find the three misspelled words. Write them correctly.

CAMP SUNRISE
July 12

7:30	Jump out of bed!	2:00	Play tennis,
8:00	Eat breakfast.		softball, or volleyball.
8:30	Make beds, sweap floor.	5:45	Dinner.
9:00	Swim or hike.	6:30	Speach and film.
12:15	Lunch.	8:00	Sing at campfire.
1:00	Quiet, pleese!	9:00	Lights out.

Verbs

7. _____   8. _____

9. _____   10. _____

11. _____   12. _____

13. _____   14. _____

Misspelled Words

15. _____   16. _____   17. _____

WORDS AT WORK

Challenge Yourself

beacon   conceal   treason   meek

Decide which Challenge Word fits each clue. Check your Spelling Dictionary to see if you were right. Then write sentences showing that you understand the meaning of each Challenge Word.

1. When you hide something, you do this to it.

2. Someone who is quiet and gentle is this.

3. If you help your country's enemies, you are guilty of this crime.

4. The light at the top of a lighthouse is one.

Write to the Point

In "Vana's Big Race," the excitement reached its peak as Vana rounded the last turn. Think about your favorite sport and write a paragraph about it. Tell what makes that sport exciting for you to play or watch. Try to use words that will interest your readers. Use spelling words from this lesson.

Challenge Use one or more of the Challenge Words in your paragraph.

Proofreading

Use the proofreading marks to show the errors in the paragraph below. Write the five misspelled words correctly in the blanks.

Did joining the track team teech me what hard work meens Yes, did! I run during every seasen. Often I either freaze melt. Some days it doesn't seem worth it. Then we win, and I remember the reeson.

◯	word is misspelled
∧	word is missing
?∧	question mark is missing

1. _____

2. _____

3. _____

4. _____

5. _____

27

Lesson 5 Months, Days, Titles

Say each spelling word.

January
February
March
April
May
June
July
August
September
October
November
December

Sunday
Monday
Tuesday
Wednesday
Thursday
Friday
Saturday

Dr.

1. Write the words that begin with the letter <u>s</u>.
_____
_____

2. Write the words that begin with the letter <u>t</u>.
_____ _____

3. Write the words that begin with a vowel.
_____ _____
_____

4. Which word begins like <u>month</u> and ends with the same three letters as <u>someday</u>?
_____

5. Which words end with the letters <u>ber</u>?
_____ _____
_____ _____

6. Which words have one syllable?
_____

7. Write the two-syllable words that have a vowel at the end of each syllable.
_____

8. Write the words that have four syllables.
_____ _____

9. Write the word in which you see the letter <u>d</u> but don't hear /d/. _____

10. Write the title abbreviation that contains only consonant letters. _____
Use the Spelling Dictionary to spell the word these two letters stand for. _____

28

Checkpoint

Write a spelling word for each clue.
Then use the Checkpoint Study Plan on page 224.

1. Halloween is in ___.

2. Most calendars start the week on ___.

3. Winter begins in ___.

4. U.S. Independence Day is the 4th of ___.

5. The last day of the school week is on ___.

6. Most calendars end the week on ___.

7. Thirty days have September, April, June, and ___.

8. The middle of the week is ___.

9. The month that comes before April is ___.

10. The first day of school each week is ___.

11. the second month of the year ___

12. The day before Friday is ___.

13. Autumn begins in ___.

14. A short way to write doctor is ___.

15. Summer begins in ___.

16. Carry an umbrella in ___.

17. The eighth month is ___.

18. the merry month of ___

19. The day after Monday is ___.

20. *Janus* was the Roman god of gates. *Janus* had
two faces, one on each side of the gate.
Because of this, he could see the people coming
in, as well as those going out. The Romans
named a month for *Janus*. It is the month that
sees the old year go out and the new year
come in. This month is the mystery word. Can
you guess it? ___

29

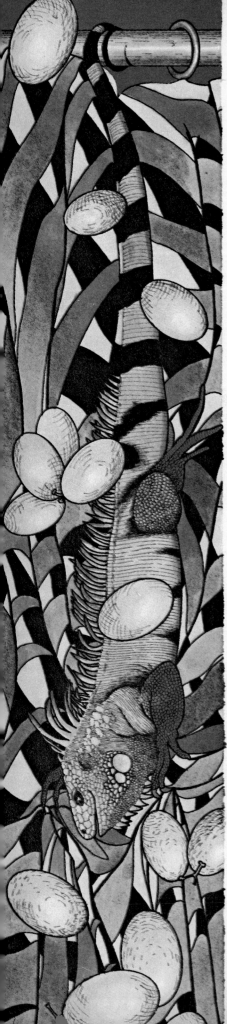

Through the Months with You

In _____, snow falls and drifts,

But I'll bring to you some warm-up gifts.

I'll bring you a cage that's warm and bright.

I'll bring you a home where everything's right.

_____ has storms and such,

But I'll give your cage that extra touch.

I'll give you a tree that you can climb,

And sand to dig when you have time.

In _____ the cold winds really blow,

So I'll take you to a lizard show.

In _____ the weather's warm but wet,

So I'll take you to see _____ Vet.

He'll look at your ears and eyes and nose.

He'll check your tail too, I suppose.

_____ has lots of pretty flowers,

So I'll build fancy flower towers.

You can climb and have some fun,

And eat the flowers one by one.

In _____ school is finally over.

I'll fill your cage with nice green clover.

In _____ the weather's hot and sticky.

To find a present might be tricky.

I'll fight for your freedom in the house.

Watch out for traps set for the mouse!

In _____ I'm a hot potato.

I'll feed you lettuce and tomato.

I'll give you meat in your salad lunch,

And maybe bananas by the bunch.

In _____ I go back to

school,

But you can play in your swimming pool.

In _____ when the leaves are

dropping,

I'll take you with me when I go shopping.

I'll let you walk around the mall,

In your new harness you'll have a ball.

In _____ we all give thanks.

You must give up playing pranks.

Remember Uncle Harry dropped the grapes,

When he saw you hanging from the drapes.

In _____ it is cold again.

I'll act just like a mother hen.

I'll let you do anything you wanna,

Because you're my dear pet iguana.

When people first named the days they named
them after their gods or heavenly bodies.

Fria's day is _____.

Thor's day is _____.

Moon's day is _____.

Woden's day is _____.

Saturn's day is _____.

Tyr's day is _____.

Sun's day is _____.

January
February
March
April
May
June
July
August
September
October
November
December
Sunday
Monday
Tuesday
Wednesday
Thursday
Friday
Saturday
Dr.

31

Capitals

Use a capital letter to begin the names of the days and months.

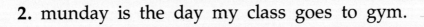Write the sentences below. Correct the spelling and capitalization of the days of the week.

1. On saturday and sonday I cook dinner.

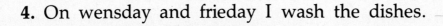

2. munday is the day my class goes to gym.

3. On toosday and thurday we have art class.

4. On wensday and frieday I wash the dishes.

Jennifer wrote this list of things for her scout group to do. She has made errors in spelling and capitalization. Write the words she misspelled correctly.

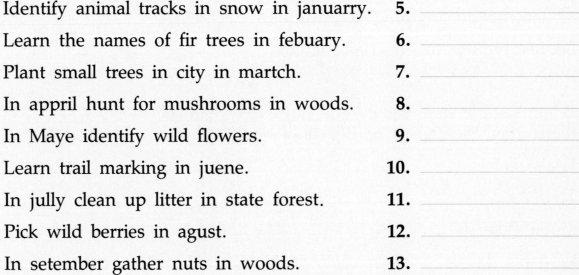

Identify animal tracks in snow in januarry.   5. _____

Learn the names of fir trees in febuary.   6. _____

Plant small trees in city in martch.   7. _____

In appril hunt for mushrooms in woods.   8. _____

In Maye identify wild flowers.   9. _____

Learn trail marking in juene.   10. _____

In jully clean up litter in state forest.   11. _____

Pick wild berries in agust.   12. _____

In setember gather nuts in woods.   13. _____

Identify types of tree leaves in oktober.   14. _____

In novimber learn animals that hibernate.   15. _____

In dicember go ice-fishing.   16. _____

Challenge Yourself

| Ms. | Pres. | Gov. | Jr. |

Use your Spelling Dictionary to answer these questions. Then write sentences showing that you understand the meaning of each Challenge Word.

1. Could someone called <u>Ms.</u> Pat Brown be a man?

2. Does the title <u>Pres.</u> before a person's name mean that the person is present?

3. What kind of job does <u>Gov.</u> Sanchez have?

4. Is Jeffrey Smith, <u>Jr.</u>, named after his father?

Write to the Point

Plan a perfect month for yourself and make all your dreams come true. Write a poem describing things you might do in that month. Make the lines rhyme as they do in the poem "Through the Months with You." Use spelling words from this lesson in your poem.

Challenge Use one or more of the Challenge Words in your poem.

Proofreading

Use the proofreading marks to show the errors in the paragraph below. Write the five misspelled words correctly in the blanks.

⬭	word is misspelled
⊙	period is missing
≡	letter should be capitalized

I got my puppy on a Monday last Awgust By Febuary he was up to my waist, and Dr. kern says he won't stop growing until Oktobur. if I buy him a big bag of dog food on Saterday, all of it is gone by Tusday

1. _____
2. _____
3. _____
4. _____
5. _____

Lesson 6 Words in Review

A. laugh
answer
banana
travel
half

B. neighbor
mistake
taste
afraid
plain
break

C. friend
guess
against
energy
sweater

D. freeze
speech
leaf
peace

★Use a piece of paper for the starred activities.

1. In Lesson 1 you studied two ways to spell /ă/: a, au. Write the words in list A.

_____ _____

_____

2. In Lesson 2 you studied four ways to spell /ā/: a_e, ai, ei, ea. Write the words in list B.

_____ _____

_____ _____

★**3.** Now write a sentence for each review word in lists A and B.

4. In Lesson 3 you studied five ways to spell /ĕ/: e, ea, ai, ie, ue. Write the words in list C.

_____ _____

_____ _____

5. In Lesson 4 you studied two ways to spell /ē/: ee, ea. Write the words in list D.

_____ _____

_____ _____

★**6.** Write the words in lists C and D. Look up each word in the Spelling Dictionary and write the guide words beside it.

★**7.** Write a sentence for the words in lists C and D.

★**8.** Write all 20 review words in alphabetical order.

Writer's Workshop

A Personal Narrative

A personal narrative is a story about something that happened to you. It might also tell how you felt about what happened. Because the story is about you, a personal narrative has pronouns like I, me, we, and my. Here is part of Tom's personal narrative about a big mistake he made.

My Biggest Mistake

I'll never forget the horrible mistake I made in my very first T-ball game. I stepped up to the plate and stared at the ball. Then I swung the bat as hard as I could. When I felt it hit the ball, I was so happy! I ran as hard and as fast as I could. On my way to the base, I saw the coach waving his arms. Oh, no! I was running to the wrong base.

To write his personal narrative, Tom followed the steps in the writing process. He began with a **Prewriting** activity to plan what he would write. Tom used a chain of events chart to list the things that happened. The chart helped him decide what to include and what to leave out. Part of Tom's chart is shown here. Study what Tom did.

1	2	3
I stepped up to the plate.	I hit the ball really hard.	I ran as fast as I could to the base.

Get ready to write your own personal narrative. It can be about your biggest mistake, your greatest moment, or any special event in your life. After you have decided what to write about, make a chain of events chart. Then follow the other steps in the writing process—**Writing, Revising, Proofreading,** and **Publishing.**

Lesson 7 Words with /ē/

Listen for /ē/ as you say each word.

easy
every
busy
city
plenty
angry
hungry
sorry
copy
family
body

police

radio
piano
ski
pizza

zebra
secret

evening

people

1. Which words begin with /s/?

_____ _____

_____ _____

2. Which words begin with a vowel?

_____ _____

_____ _____

3. Which words end with the letter <u>a</u> and have two syllables? _____

_____

4. Which words end with a vowel and have three syllables? _____

_____ _____

5. Write the words in which you see the letter <u>c</u> but hear /s/. _____

_____ _____

6. Write the words in which you see the letter <u>c</u> but hear /k/. _____

_____

7. Write the word in which the double consonant spells /t/ and /s/. _____

8. Which words have /ng/? _____

_____ _____

9. Which word begins and ends like <u>party</u>?

_____

10. Which words begin and end like <u>buddy</u>?

_____ _____

11. Solve this puzzle:

pea − a + o + ple = _____

Checkpoint

Write a spelling word for each clue.
Then use the Checkpoint Study Plan on page 224.

1. When we've had enough, we've had ____.

2. A working person is a body that's ____.

3. Spots are to leopard as stripes are to ____.

4. Another word for simple is ____.

5. The opposite of pleased is ____.

6. To go without food is to go ____.

7. not morning, but ____

8. The hardest thing to keep is a ____.

9. Men, women, and children are ____.

10. Branch is to tree as arm is to ____.

11. When she warms a pie, she heats a ____.

12. Another word for each is ____.

13. To feel pity is to feel ____.

14. Laws are enforced by the ____.

15. Ice is to skate as snow is to ____.

16. You can hear music over the ____.

17. Parents and children are a ____.

18. You'll find tall buildings in a ____.

19. A messy twin is a sloppy ____.

20. This mystery word is the name of a musical instrument. This instrument was first made in Italy. It could be played both softly and loudly. So it became known by the Italian name *pianoforte*. *Pianoforte* means soft and loud. Soon, this name was shortened to the mystery word. Can you guess it? ____

37

Gooberville

❊ WANT ADS ❊

Phil Goode Health Club and School of
_____ Building needs teacher for push-up
and jump-rope class. Help _____
tone up lazy bodies. Must carry tired customers
home. Good working hours: seven days a week
and one _____.
Call: I. M. Phitt

Pop's _____
Parlor needs cook who
can sing. Must prepare
pizza and play
_____.
Must not be afraid to
sing to
_____
crowd. We are
_____
to reach by bus or
train. Call: I. E. Talot.

_____
seeks someone to teach
pet _____
good stable manners.
Must really love lizards,
bats, elephants, and
other house pets. Send
a _____ of a
letter from some
animal you have
taught. Be sure it is
signed with a clear
paw print.

SUPER SLEUTH SEEKS SUPPORT

_____ spy
seeks helper. Must be
able to keep a
_____.
_____
of interesting work. Be
prepared to work
nights and
_____
Saturday and Sunday.
Office near center of
_____,
can't tell where. Tell
why you want the job
on self-destructing
tape and send to:
Post Office Box 11.

❊ FOR SALE ❊

Skiers: Security and Safety on the Slopes

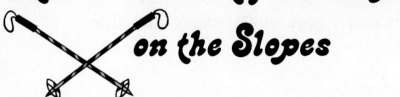

Don't be _____ when you ski. Six pairs of no-accident _____ poles for sale. Call us before Friday and get free book, Study Guide to Skiing Safety, and free pass to any hospital of your choice.

RADIO FOR SALE

Old AM _____: first broadcasting set ever used in country. Ugly frame but perfect working shape. Even picks up stations from Antarctica, messages to _____ cars, and voices of neighbors talking in their yards. For more about this offer, call: _____ neighbors of U.R.N. Eavesdropper.

easy
every
busy
city
plenty
angry
hungry
sorry
copy
family
body
police
radio
piano
ski
pizza
zebra
secret
evening
people

Commas

Use a comma (,) to separate a series of words or word groups.

Dave has a cat, a dog, and a hamster.

*On our vacation we rode in a car, flew in plane,
and sailed in a boat.*

⭐ Write the sentences below, adding commas where they are needed.

1. I told the secret to Amy Kit and Ed.

_____

2. I love music so much that I play violin piano and flute.

_____

3. At the zoo we saw a zebra an elephant and a lion.

_____

4. I like pizza with cheese peppers and onions.

_____

5. The busy city has plenty of people cars buses and traffic!

_____

6. Everyone in my family likes to ski snowshoe and skate.

_____

7. I'm sorry you lost your book pen and ruler.

_____

8. Ron Pete and Dave are angry because I missed the game.

_____

Challenge Yourself

attorney barrier retrieve fatigue

What do you think each underlined Challenge Word means? Check your Spelling Dictionary to see if you are right. Then write sentences showing that you understand the meaning of each Challenge Word.

1. We asked an attorney for advice about the law.

2. The city built a barrier to keep snow off the road.

3. Enrique has trained his dog to retrieve baseballs from the pond.

4. Although I was very tired, I didn't let my fatigue keep me from my daily jog.

Write to the Point

Advertising can be a great way to let people know what you want to sell or buy. Write an ad for something you want to buy or sell. Your ad can be silly, like the ones in this lesson, or it can be real. Be sure to give important information as well as interesting details. Use spelling words from this lesson in your ad.

Challenge Use one or more of the Challenge Words in your ad.

Proofreading

Use the proofreading marks to show the errors in the paragraph below. Write the five misspelled words correctly in the blanks.

	word is misspelled
≡	letter should be capitalized
∼	take out word

A yard sale is a an eazy way for a familiy to sell things. just make a sign and put it a copie at evry corner. Have the sale on a saturday so that plenty of poeple can come.

1. _____

2. _____

3. _____

4. _____

5. _____

Lesson 8   Words with /ĭ/

Listen for /ĭ/ as you say each word.

deliver

quick

interesting

picnic

thick

chicken

itch

pitch

begin

inch

bridge

written

middle

picture

different

village

package

building

guitar

gym

1. Which words end with /k/? _____

_____   _____

2. Write the other words in which you hear /k/.

_____   _____

_____

3. Which words end with the letters ch?

_____

_____

4. Write the word in which you see the letter w but don't hear /w/. _____

5. Write the word in which you hear /kw/.

_____

6. Write the word in which /d/ is spelled dd.

_____

7. Write the words in which you hear /j/ but don't see the letter j. _____

_____

_____

8. Which words have the same spelling of /ĭ/ as built? _____

_____

9. Which word begins and ends like been?

_____

10. Which words begin with a vowel?

_____   _____

_____

11. Which words begin with the letter d?

_____   _____

Checkpoint

Write a spelling word for each clue.
Then use the Checkpoint Study Plan on page 224.

1. I write, I have ___.
2. Another word for start is ___.
3. Chicken pox or poison ivy makes you ___.
4. between the beginning and ending ___
5. Another word for bundle is ___.
6. Many people work in an office ___.
7. to take a letter to someone ___
8. When you get to the river, cross that ___.
9. a place where one exercises ___
10. A six-stringed instrument is a ___.
11. Draw a line that measures one ___.
12. not dull, but ___
13. Another word for fast is ___.
14. A hen or a rooster is a ___.
15. The opposite of thin is ___.
16. pretty as a ___
17. not the same, but ___
18. If you throw a baseball, you ___.
19. Ship is to boat as city is to ___.

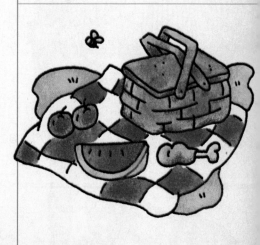

20. This mystery word names a meal eaten outside. It came from a French word. The word it came from was *piquenique*. Recently, the Japanese borrowed the word from English. They call an outside meal a *pikunikku*. Can you guess what we call this meal? ___

43

SCRAMBLED PLANS

Tommy was flying the family spaceship when he saw the lights on the panel _____ to flash.

He called out to his sister, "Nancy, the ship is on a _____ course!"

The rocket landed with a "Bump!" The children saw that they were in the _____ of a group of houses. Each _____ looked exactly like a giant _____ coop. It was a whole _____ of chicken coops!

As the children climbed out of the ship, they noticed a flying figure coming toward them. _____ as a flash, a five-foot one- _____ chicken stood in their path. He was taller than Tommy and had a _____ covering of white feathers.

"Welcome, children," he said clearly in English. "We've been EGGS-PECK-ting you!"

"What do you want of us?" the children asked.

"Our great-grandchickens left your planet in search of freedom from the boiling pot. They took a _____ record of Earth's most _____ sports. But somehow, we lost the game of baseball!"

44

"And you want us to teach you?" Nancy asked.

"EGGS-actly. And once we learn, we will

_____ you safely back to Earth."

The children agreed and the chicken spread his wings with delight. Soon, they were off! They crossed over a _____ and walked until they reached the school _____. Here, the children taught the chickens the lost art of baseball. Nancy worked on the _____ and Tommy worked on the hit.

That evening, the chicken planet held its first baseball game. Everyone brought _____ suppers. Someone played a _____. Soon the score was tied 3–all. Everyone was excited. The pitcher was chewing gum and scratching an _____ on his bill. A high fly over the head of a left-field chicken ended the game. Nancy was flown off the diamond by a cheering crowd while Tommy snapped a picture. He wanted proof that the planet was real.

The children were returned to Earth, as the chickens had promised. But months later, a

_____ came from the chicken planet. It was a baseball signed with chicken scratches. They wished they could take it to school with the _____. But the picture hadn't developed. They knew that no one would believe them. So they put the ball away in a box with their best belongings.

deliver
quick
interesting
picnic
thick
chicken
itch
pitch
begin
inch
bridge
written
middle
picture
different
village
package
building
guitar
gym

45

Syllables

The words listed and explained in a dictionary are called entry words. An entry word in the dictionary is divided into syllables.

> **syl·la·ble** | sĭl′ə′bəl | *n.*   A single uninterrupted sound forming part of a word or in some cases an entire word.

★ These are examples of entry words. Count how many syllables each word has and write down the number.

1. chick•en _____   **2.** pitch _____   **3.** de•liv•er _____

★ Find each of the words below in the Spelling Dictionary. Write them in syllables, putting a dot between the syllables.

4. guitar _____   **5.** village _____

Sometimes words are started on one line and finished on the next. This is done by dividing a word into syllables and putting a hyphen at the end of the word part on the first line.

> *I'll never forgive my father for taking a pic-*
> *ture of me when I had the mumps.*

★ Bill wrote this article for his school newspaper. It had to fit the narrow columns. He made mistakes in syllabication. Look in the Spelling Dictionary. Write the words with correct syllable breaks.

Come one! Come all!
Our school's annual spring picnic will be held this Saturday.
A list of events will be writt-
en on the board in the middl-
e lobby of the school building. Relay races are to begin at noon and eight different refreshment stands will be
in the yard for your enjoyment!

6. _____

7. _____
8. _____
9. _____
10. _____
11. _____

46

Challenge Yourself

dismal   **banish**
       Gypsy   **acknowledge**

What do you think each underlined Challenge Word means? Check your Spelling Dictionary to see if you are right. Then write sentences showing that you understand the meaning of each Challenge Word.

1. We wanted Saturday to be sunny, but the weather was <u>dismal</u>.

2. The king decided to <u>banish</u> all thieves to an island.

3. Elisa is a <u>Gypsy</u>, but her family no longer travels from place to place as her grandparents did.

4. The spaceship captain would not <u>acknowledge</u> that they were lost.

Write to the Point

Imagine that you meet a creature from another planet. What does the creature look like? How does it sound? What does it do? Write a description of the visitor. Describe how it moves about. Tell if the creature seems friendly and what makes you think so. Use spelling words from this lesson in your description.

Challenge Use one or more of the Challenge Words in your description.

Proofreading

Use the proofreading marks to show the errors in the paragraph below. Write the five misspelled words correctly in the blanks.

⬭	word is misspelled
⊙	period is missing
∧	word is missing

It landed by the brige in the middel the day. It looked like a bilding and puffed thick green smoke into the air I tried take a pichur, but I wasn't quik enough.

1. _____

2. _____

3. _____

4. _____

5. _____

Lesson 9　Words with /ī/

Listen for /ī/ as you say each word.

fight

right

might

sight

bright

high

highway

lightning

tonight

midnight

flight

night

mighty

deny

reply

supply

spy

dry

die

tie

1. Which word begins and ends like <u>net</u>?

   _____

2. Which word begins and ends like <u>brat</u>?

   _____

3. Which word begins like <u>rate</u> and ends with the same four letters as <u>light</u>? _____

4. Which word begins like <u>sink</u> and ends with the same four letters as <u>fright</u>? _____

5. Which word begins and ends with the letter <u>t</u>?

   _____

6. Which words contain only one consonant?

   _____　_____

7. Write the one-syllable words in which /ī/ is spelled <u>y</u>. _____

   _____

8. Write the two-syllable words in which /ī/ is spelled <u>y</u>. _____

   _____　_____

9. Which word begins with the letter <u>l</u> and has two syllables? _____

10. Write the compound word that begins with the letter <u>h</u>.

    _____

11. Write the remaining words in which /ī/ is spelled <u>igh</u>. _____　_____

    _____　_____

    _____　_____

48

Checkpoint

Write a spelling word for each clue.
Then use the Checkpoint Study Plan on page 224.

1. The opposite of wrong is ___.

2. not last night, but ___

3. Riding in a jet after dark is a night ___.

4. Arguing in the dark is a night ___.

5. When both hands point to twelve, it is ___.

6. Another word for shiny is ___.

7. To fasten with rope is to ___.

8. as fast as greased ___

9. The opposite of to live is to ___.

10. Another word for strong is ___.

11. Being able to see means you have ___.

12. The opposite of low is ___.

13. Someone who steals secrets is a ___.

14. To answer someone is to ___.

15. Dark is to light as wet is to ___.

16. not day, but ___

17. To say it's a lie is to ___.

18. Another word for give is ___.

19. wish I may, wish I ___

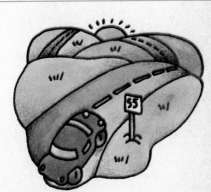

20. Long ago in England, there were certain important roads or <u>ways</u>. Small roads were called <u>byways</u>. Most of the main roads were built <u>higher</u> than the ground around them. They had a <u>different</u> name than the other ways. That name is the mystery word. Can you guess it? ___

49

Dinosaurs Yesterday

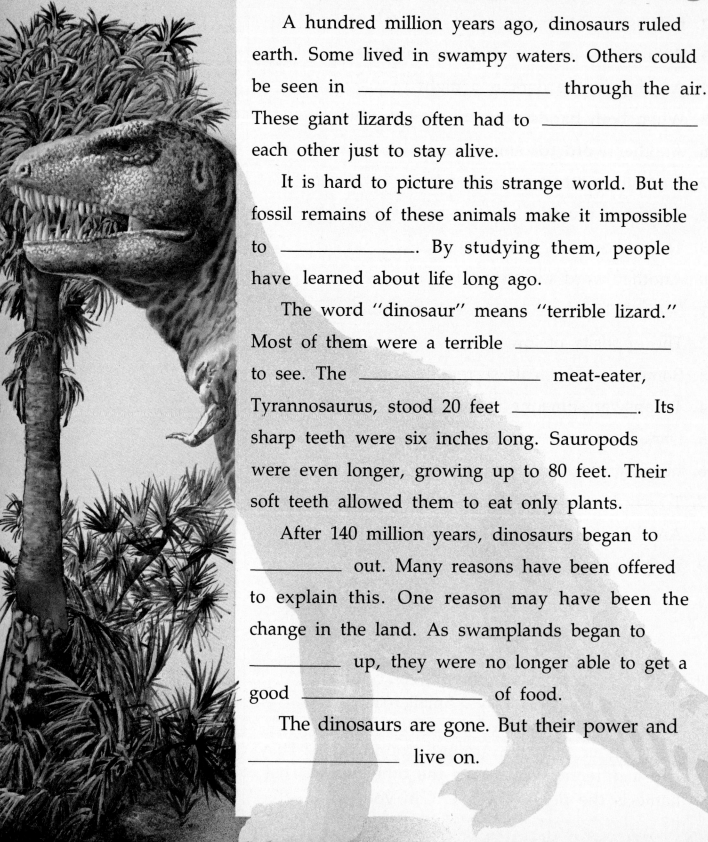

A hundred million years ago, dinosaurs ruled earth. Some lived in swampy waters. Others could be seen in _____ through the air. These giant lizards often had to _____ each other just to stay alive.

It is hard to picture this strange world. But the fossil remains of these animals make it impossible to _____. By studying them, people have learned about life long ago.

The word "dinosaur" means "terrible lizard." Most of them were a terrible _____ to see. The _____ meat-eater, Tyrannosaurus, stood 20 feet _____. Its sharp teeth were six inches long. Sauropods were even longer, growing up to 80 feet. Their soft teeth allowed them to eat only plants.

After 140 million years, dinosaurs began to _____ out. Many reasons have been offered to explain this. One reason may have been the change in the land. As swamplands began to _____ up, they were no longer able to get a good _____ of food.

The dinosaurs are gone. But their power and _____ live on.

...And Today

The _____ light was shining through the window as Mom and I pulled into the lot. Once again, Dad was working through the _____. We were bringing him his _____ dinner. Walking through those empty halls, I felt like a _____.

But _____ was important. Dad was finishing his work on "Old Meggie."

When we arrived, a 12-foot frame of the Megalosaurus greeted us. "Old Meggie" had been Dad's work for two years. I always wondered why he chose to be a paleontologist. Whenever I asked him why he'd bother putting together a stack of old bones, he'd _____ jokingly, "To _____ together pieces of the past."

Then he'd say, "To learn about the changes that took place on earth."

We hardly noticed the loud thunder and the bright _____ as we took a _____ turn onto the empty _____ that night. We were all so happy that Dad's work was done! Our midnight rides were over — for a while.

fight
right
might
sight
bright
high
highway
lightning
tonight
midnight
flight
night
mighty
deny
reply
supply
spy
dry
die
tie

51

Entry Words

Often, two dictionaries will treat an entry word in different ways.

⭐ These entries for the word <u>night</u> come from two dictionaries.

A **night** | nīt | —*noun, plural* **nights** **1.** The time between sunset and sunrise, especially the hours of darkness. **2.** The part of the night when people sleep or rest: *He tossed and turned all night.* ♦ *These sound alike* **night, knight.**

B **night** | nīt | *n.* **1.** The period between sunset and sunrise, especially the hours of darkness. **2.** The part of the night devoted to sleep or rest: *He tossed and turned all night.* **3.** An evening or night devoted to some special purpose or event: *the opening night of a play.* **4.** Nightfall: *They worked from morning to night* **5.** Darkness: *She ran out into the foggy night.* **6.** Any gloomy time of inactivity, sorrow, ignorance, or evil: *a long night of waiting before our dreams come true.* —**modifier:** *the night air; a night nurse.* These sound alike **night, knight** .

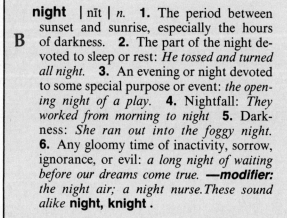

1. How many meanings does entry A show for <u>night</u>? _____

2. How many meanings does entry B show for <u>night</u>? _____

3. Which entry shows the plural form, <u>nights</u>? _____

⭐ Some entry words have more than one meaning. Look at entry B. List the definition number which gives the meaning of the word <u>night</u> as it is used in each sentence below.

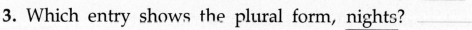

4. The car drove off into the night. _____

5. The mayor attended the opening night game. _____

6. During the winter, it becomes dark early in the night. _____

7. It is hard to sleep at night in my house. _____

⭐ Write the following words. Then look them up in the Spelling Dictionary. Write the number of meanings each word has.

bright   flight   spy

8. _____   9. _____   10. _____

Challenge Yourself

eyesight   untimely
     dignify   quietness

Use your Spelling Dictionary to answer these questions. Then write sentences showing that you understand the meaning of each Challenge Word.

1. Would excellent <u>eyesight</u> be needed to see a dinosaur standing a few feet away?

2. Does an <u>untimely</u> event occur at the wrong time?

3. If you want to <u>dignify</u> friends, should you make fun of them?

4. Does <u>quietness</u> keep most people from falling asleep?

Write to the Point

Suppose you are a scientist and you discover an island where dinosaurs still live. Use your imagination to write a journal entry about your first day on the island. What kinds of strange things did you see? Use spelling words from this lesson in your journal entry.

Challenge Use one or more of the Challenge Words in your journal entry.

Proofreading

Use the proofreading marks to show the errors in the paragraph below. Write the five misspelled words correctly in the blanks.

| word is misspelled |
| period is missing |
| letter should be capitalized |

dinah, the museum's cement dinosaur, stands by the hyway She is two stories hi and painted brite green. at night no one can denie that she looks real Dinah is one dinosaur that will never dye.

1. _____

2. _____

3. _____

4. _____

5. _____

Lesson 10 Words with /ī/

Listen for /ī/ as you say each word.

life

knife

slide

beside

twice

wise

size

surprise

write

smile

sunshine

awhile

quiet

iron

child

behind

blind

climb

giant

buy

1. Which words end with /d/?

_____

_____

_____

2. Which words end with /z/? _____

_____

3. Which words begin with a vowel?

_____

4. Write the two-syllable words in which a vowel ends the first syllable and a vowel begins the second syllable. _____

_____

5. Write the word in which you see the letter k but don't hear /k/. _____

6. Write the word in which you see the letter w but don't hear /w/. _____

7. Write the word in which you see the letter b but don't hear /b/. _____

8. Write the word in which /s/ is spelled with the letter c. _____

9. Which word begins like smell and ends with the same three letters as file? _____

10. Which word begins like line and ends with the same three letters as wife? _____

11. Write the compound word that begins with the letter s. _____

12. Which word has the same spelling of /ī/ as guy?

_____

54

Checkpoint

Write a spelling word for each clue.
Then use the Checkpoint Study Plan on page 224.

1. not once, but ____

2. not an adult, but a ____

3. Moon is to moonlight as sun is to ____.

4. Another word for smart is ____.

5. For a short time means ____.

6. Another word for grin is ____.

7. The opposite of noisy is ____.

8. not sell, but ____

9. This coat is the right ____.

10. Voice is to speak as pen and paper are to ____.

11. something you do to a mountain or ladder ____

12. Small is to tiny as huge is to ____.

13. One hard metal is called ____.

14. fork, spoon, and ____

15. The opposite of death is ____.

16. not in front of, but ____

17. Close your eyes to get a ____.

18. Next to means ____.

19. slip and ____

20. Sometimes a group of words all come from the
    same root. These words are said to be related.
    This mystery word is related to many other
    words. It is related to the Viking word *blunda*.
    Blunda meant to close one's eyes in sleep. The
    mystery word means that a person can't see.
    Can you guess the mystery word? ____

55

How Coyote Helped to Light the World

Long ago, when there was no light anywhere, a coyote tried to climb up a mountain. Each time he tried, he would _____ down and then _____ back up again. At last, he made it to the top. There, to his _____, Coyote felt a "bump" against his nose.

"Sorry, I didn't see you there," said a hawk.

"It's so dark," said Coyote, "that I didn't see you, either."

The two sat _____ each other and talked about how wonderful the world would be with light. They rested _____. It grew very _____ and still. Then Coyote, who was very _____, began to _____.

"I will gather straw and roll it into a ball," said Coyote. "Then I'll bring you pieces of flint. You must take them and fly high up in the sky. Then, light the ball of straw and fly away quickly."

And so the hawk took the ball and the flint and flew as high as he could fly. He struck the flint together. Once, _____, and the sparks began to fly. They caught the straw in a blaze of light that lit the world.

56

Hawk thought that the bright light would make him _____. So he flew back to earth, and turned back to look _____ him at the _____ flame he left burning in the sky. Below, for the first time, Hawk could see the wonders of _____: trees, lakes, and animals, each one a different shape and a different _____.

Coyote and Hawk were so happy with the _____ that they decided to light the night sky. This time Coyote gathered straw that was damp. When Hawk lit the ball, only a pale light appeared. And so the moon was made.

Coyote felt such sorrow at the pale light of the moon that he howled all through the night. And even today, coyotes can be heard howling because the moon is too dim!

1. Many years ago folktales were told by an adult to a _____.

2. A story would be passed by word-of-mouth until someone decided to _____ it down.

3. Coyote and Hawk wanted to light the world. Their will was as strong as _____.

4. Coyote's claws cut like a _____.

5. The sun and the moon are things that money can't _____.

57

life
knife
slide
beside
twice
wise
size
surprise
write
smile
sunshine
awhile
quiet
iron
child
behind
blind
climb
giant
buy

Nouns

A noun is a word that names a person, place, thing, or idea.

child   park   toy   happiness

 ⭐ Find the noun in each group of words and write it down.

 1. life   wise   behind

2. beside   teach   smile

 3. knife   over   swam

4. up   child   ran

 5. low   iron   before

6. quick   until   sunshine

7. surprise   last   awhile

8. after   at   size

 ⭐ Sammy and Sarah each have their own household chores. This week Sarah asked Sammy to swap chores. She wrote this note to Sammy, but made four spelling mistakes. Write a list of the nouns in this note and correct Sarah's misspelled words. (Write each noun only once.)

The soap powder and the bleach are behinde the napkins on the bottom shelf. You may have to by more bleach. Remember to separate the towels from the jeans. Run the towels through the dryer twise. See you later and thanks again.

S.

P.S. Don't bleach the jeans, wize guy!

	Nouns	Misspelled Words
9.	13.	17.
10.	14.	18.
11.	15.	19.
12.	16.	20.

Challenge Yourself

acquire   collide   defiant   revive

What do you think each underlined Challenge Word means? Check your Spelling Dictionary to see if you are right. Then write sentences showing that you understand the meaning of each Challenge Word.

1. Andy needs to earn money in order to <u>acquire</u> a new bicycle.

2. The hall is so crowded that students sometimes <u>collide</u>.

3. Renotta thought her dog was <u>defiant</u> because he would not <u>follow</u> her commands.

4. The droopy flowers began to <u>revive</u> after the rain.

Write to the Point

Like the Coyote story you read, many stories explain how or why things came to be the way they are on earth. Write your own "how" or "why" story. For example, you could explain how the turtle got its shell or how the cactus got its needles. Use spelling words from this lesson in your story.

Challenge Use one or more of the Challenge Words in your story.

Proofreading

Use the proofreading marks to show the errors in the paragraph below. Write the five misspelled words correctly in the blanks.

What i am about to rite may surprize you. Mice are not quiet, owls are not wize, and cats do not have nine lives. It is true, though, that elephants giunt in size, and snakes slied on the ground.

◯	word is misspelled
=	letter should be capitalized
∧	word is missing

1. _____

2. _____

3. _____

4. _____

5. _____

Lesson 11 Plurals

Say each spelling word.

brothers

trees

pockets

rocks

hikes

gloves

dishes

classes

brushes

inches

branches

peaches

buses

foxes

boxes

stories

babies

cities

pennies

families

Solve these plural puzzles.

train + s = <u>trains</u>

1. brother + s = _____

2. tree + s = _____

3. pocket + s = _____

4. glove + s = _____

5. rock + s = _____

6. hike + s = _____

match + es = <u>matches</u>

7. dish + es = _____

8. inch + es = _____

9. bus + es = _____

10. fox + es = _____

11. branch + es = _____

12. brush + es = _____

13. peach + es = _____

14. class + es = _____

15. box + es = _____

buddy − y + i + es = <u>buddies</u>

16. city − y + i + es = _____

17. baby − y + i + es = _____

18. story − y + i + es = _____

19. penny − y + i + es = _____

20. family − y + i + es = _____

Checkpoint

Write a spelling word for each clue.
Then use the Checkpoint Study Plan on page 224.

1. Girls are to sisters as boys are to ____.

2. Kangaroos have pouches. Jackets have ____.

3. To get promoted, a student passes ____.

4. Tracks are to trains as roads are to ____.

5. Fingers are to hands as twigs are to ____.

6. as sly as ____

7. Granite and limestone are kinds of ____.

8. Plates are also called ____.

9. Feet are to socks as hands are to ____.

10. Another word for walks is ____.

11. not combs, but ____

12. New York and Los Angeles are ____.

13. another word for cents ____

14. not adults, but ____

15. Cereal is packed in ____.

16. can't see the forest for the ____

17. One-sixth of a foot is two ____.

18. parents and children ____

19. tales and legends ____

20. This mystery word is the name of a fruit. The Romans called this fruit a Persian apple, or *persicum malum*. Later it was simply called *persicum*. The French changed the word to *pesche*. It is from *pesche* that the mystery word came into English. Guess the name of this fruit. Add the plural <u>es</u> to form the mystery word. ____

61

Use each spelling word once.

A Dream Come True

I'd always wanted to climb Franconia Notch. I'd taken _____ in mountain climbing and had gone up small peaks with my _____. Now, I was going to climb the White Mountains.

George, Mike, and I left early, driving through neighboring _____ and towns. Finally, we arrived! I heard the hum of motors as cars and _____ carried people to the mountain's base.

Mike said, "Come on, Small Fry."

I went, but I wanted to tell him I was tired of being called Small Fry.

We took our _____ off and strapped ourselves together. I was between Mike and George because I could not see.

The climb began well. In the beginning, the tree _____ felt like the bristles of _____ against my face. Mike told me about the animals he saw: some _____ and two _____ of rabbits! I heard screeching sounds, and George said that it was a red-tailed hawk. We figured that her _____ were in a nest nearby.

We stopped to rest on a ledge and told

_____ about other _____

we'd taken. We opened the small _____

of raisins and nuts. Mike took out the three

_____ he'd packed and we

began eating.

"One good thing about this lunch is that we

don't have to wash any _____,"

I joked.

We began to climb again. There were no more

_____, just hard rock. Suddenly, the

_____ crumbled beneath me and I fell. I

lost all sense of where I was and tried to grab on

to something.

"You O.K.?" George asked, holding the rope.

"Just a few more _____ up with

your right foot," Mike shouted.

At last, I was able to get my footing again.

"Some rock slide," yelled Mike. "That was nice

work, Nick!"

The rest of the way to the top was easier. I

searched my _____ for the three

lucky _____ that George had

given me, knowing that it was more than luck that

got us to the top.

Somehow, I knew, too, that I would never be

"Small Fry" again.

brothers
trees
pockets
rocks
hikes
gloves
dishes
classes
brushes
inches
branches
peaches
buses
foxes
boxes
stories
babies
cities
pennies
families

Subject of a Sentence

The subject is the part of a sentence that is doing the action or is being talked about. To find the subject, first find the verb. Then ask who or what did the action described by the verb. The answer will be the subject of the sentence.

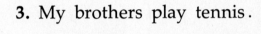

The brave soldiers marched by the palace.

<u>Marched</u> is the verb, so <u>the brave soldiers</u> is the subject of the sentence.

 ★ Write the subject of each sentence.

1. Peaches grow in my grandmother's front yard.

_____

2. My pockets ripped.

_____

3. My brothers play tennis.

_____

4. Dance classes begin at three o'clock.

_____

5. The oak trees lost their leaves in October.

_____

6. Many tree branches fell during the storm.

_____

7. The red foxes hid in their den with their mother.

_____

8. Many new families moved to our neighborhood this year.

_____

9. Two cardboard boxes tumbled off the shelf.

_____

10. One of our best dishes broke.

_____

WORDS AT WORK

Challenge Yourself

utensils	draperies
skiers	festivities

What do you think each underlined Challenge Word means? Check your Spelling Dictionary to see if you are right. Then write sentences showing that you understand the meaning of each Challenge Word.

1. Fog hid the mountain like draperies covering a window.

2. Many skiers race down the mountain slopes after it snows.

3. We had only a pan, knife, and spoon for cooking utensils.

4. The festivities on the last day of school included singing and a special meal.

Write to the Point

Nick's mountain climb had some scary moments, but afterward he was proud. Have you ever learned how to do something that was scary at first? Maybe you learned to ride a bike or swim. Write a paragraph about what it was like to be a beginner. What happened? How did you feel? Use spelling words from this lesson in your paragraph.

Challenge Use one or more of the Challenge Words in your paragraph.

Proofreading

Use the proofreading marks to show the errors in the paragraph below. Write the five misspelled words correctly in the blanks.

⬭	word is misspelled
⊙	period is missing
⟿	take out word

Like most kids in citys, I can't take many hikes in in the woods, so I go to a park. There I enjoy the tres and climb a the rockes   One day I saw two foxs and their babys.

1. _____

2. _____

3. _____

4. _____

5. _____

Lesson 12 Words in Review

A. evening
family
secret
radio
police
people

B. pitch
interesting
different
gym
package
building

C. lightning
flight
supply
buy
surprise
quiet
giant
tie

★Use a piece of paper for the starred activities.

1. In Lesson 7 you studied six ways to spell /ē/: y, i_e, i, e, e_e, eo. Write the words in list A.

_____   _____

_____   _____

2. In Lesson 8 you studied four ways to spell /ĭ/: i, a, ui, y. Write the words in list B.

_____   _____

_____   _____

_____   _____

★**3.** Write the words in lists A and B. Look up each word in the Spelling Dictionary and divide it into syllables.

4. In Lessons 9 and 10 you studied five ways to spell /ī/: i, y, ie, i_e, uy. Write the words in list C.

_____   _____

_____   _____

_____   _____

★**5.** Now write a sentence for each review word in list C. Make four statements that end with periods. Make two questions and two sentences that end with exclamation points.

★**6.** Divide the words in list C into syllables.

★**7.** Write all 20 review words in alphabetical order.

66

Writer's Workshop

A Narrative

A narrative is a story. It can be a true story or a made-up one. A made-up story is called <u>fiction</u>. It comes from the writer's imagination. The writer of a narrative tries to grab the reader's interest at the beginning of the story. Then the writer often keeps the reader wondering what will happen next. Here is the beginning of Koji's story about a boy who loses his brother's skateboard.

The Lost Skateboard

It was the most wonderful skateboard Matt had ever seen. It was shiny red, and the wheels spun quietly and smoothly. Matt's big brother Andy had been given the skateboard for his birthday only last week.

"Can I borrow your skateboard?" Matt asked.

"I guess so. Just make sure you don't let anything happen to it," Andy said.

To write his narrative, Koji followed the steps in the writing process. He began with a **Prewriting** activity using a story map. The story map helped Koji plan his narrative. He wrote down each important event that would take place in the story. Part of Koji's story map is shown here. Study what Koji did.

> **Beginning**
>
> Matt borrows big brother's new skateboard

> **Middle**
>
> Matt leaves skateboard on the bus

Get ready to write your own narrative. You can write a story like Koji's, a fairy tale, or any other kind of story you wish. Once you have an idea for your story, make a story map to plan the main events. Then follow the other steps in the writing process—**Writing, Revising, Proofreading,** and **Publishing.**

Lesson 13 Words with /ŏ/

Listen for /ŏ/ as you say each word.

beyond

forgot

doctor

o'clock

cotton

solve

model

problem

knot

knock

bottom

hospital

dollar

contest

hobby

object

wash

wallet

watch

swallow

1. Which words begin with /w/? _____

_____

2. Write the words that begin with a vowel. Circle the word that has an apostrophe.

_____ _____

3. Write the words that begin with /k/.

_____ _____

4. Write the words that begin with /n/.

_____ _____

5. Write the word in which /b/ is spelled bb.

_____

6. Write the two-syllable words that have the same vowel in both syllables. _____

_____ _____

7. Which word begins and ends like motel? _____

8. Which word begins and ends like program? _____

9. Which word ends with the same three letters as pond? _____

10. Which word ends with the same four letters as revolve? _____

11. Which words have ll? _____

_____

12. Which word has three syllables? _____

Checkpoint

Write a spelling word for each clue.
Then use the Checkpoint Study Plan on page 224.

1. Today I forget, yesterday I ____.

2. "You are ill. Don't get a chill," says the ____.

3. His name is Bill, but he's not worth a ____.

4. A case for money and pictures is a ____.

5. Another word for thing is ____.

6. Collecting old coins or stamps is a ____.

7. Ted said, "The time is now two ____."

8. Don't tie your shoelaces in a ____.

9. That 10-foot pizza story was hard to ____.

10. On the far side of means ____.

11. "Who's there?" jokes begin with knock, ____.

12. not the solution, but the ____

13. To clean with water means to ____.

14. Another word for race is ____.

15. The opposite of top is ____.

16. Rough is to wool as soft is to ____.

17. To look at means to ____.

18. His plastic airplane was a scale ____.

19. The detective had a hard case to ____.

20. *Hospitium* was a Latin word that meant a house for guests. Long ago, monks ran rest houses for travelers. The rest houses took their name from the word *hospitium*. Weary people stopped at the rest houses to get food and rest. The mystery word also comes from *hospitium*. It names a place where sick people go to get well. Can you guess it? ____

69

A Hobby for Kim

My sister just built a _____ of a ship. Building models is her _____. My brother likes to work with leather. He made a beautiful _____ last week. Dad gave him a _____ to put in it. Dad was happy because he finally won a _____. He's always entering them. I thought the contest he won was silly. Dad wrote 25 words about why he likes to do the _____ with new, blue Cleano. And Mom? She likes to _____ birds. She was very excited Monday when she saw a _____.

I'm the only one in my family who doesn't have a hobby. Everyone else has one thing he or she loves to do. My family teases me about not having a hobby. They say, "Kim doesn't know what she likes." The trouble is I like everything. As soon as I begin to do one thing, something else also seems interesting. It seems a shame to spend all my time on one activity. There are so many interesting things to do. Finding a hobby has been a real _____. I even got into a "scrape" trying to _____ this problem.

Yesterday I thought skating might be my hobby. I was rolling down Holly Hill and had just picked up speed. I was almost certain I could spend all my free time skating. The wind felt wonderful against my face. Then I saw someone in the park flying a kite. It was made of bright blue paper. Red _____ tails were waving below it. Each tail had a _____ tied in it. I _____ about skating. I thought how much fun flying kites would be as a hobby. Before I knew it, I was at the _____ of the hill. Just _____ the bottom is a sharp turn. Well, the road turned but I didn't. CRASH! My knee got quite a _____.

Mom wasn't too happy when the police officer called her at two _____. She left her office and met us at the _____. At first she was angry with me. Then she told me she was only angry because she was frightened. She felt better when she knew I would be all right. The _____ cleaned my cut and bandaged my knee. She told me to wash my knee with special medicine. I didn't _____. My knee hurt and I wanted it to get better.

It was an exciting day, though. I got to see lots of doctors and nurses. The inside of a hospital is really interesting. I told the doctor how much I liked visiting the hospital. Mom couldn't stop laughing when the doctor said, ''Just don't make it a hobby!''

71

beyond
forgot
doctor
o'clock
cotton
solve
model
problem
knot
knock
bottom
hospital
dollar
contest
hobby
object
wash
wallet
watch
swallow

Parts of Speech

A dictionary lists the part of speech for each entry word. For example, a word may be a noun (n.) or a verb (v.).

★ Write the following words in alphabetical order. Look up each word in the Spelling Dictionary and write its part of speech.

forgot   solve   hospital   hobby

Word	Part of Speech
1.	
2.	
3.	
4.	

Some words are used as more than one part of speech. A dictionary lists the most commonly used part of speech first. Then the other parts of speech and definitions are listed.

★ Look at the entries for object[1] and object[2].

5. In which entry (1 or 2) does object mean "to argue"? _____

6. What part of speech is object[1]? _____
object[2]? _____

7. Write two sentences using object as each part of speech.

---

ob·ject[1] | ŏb′jĭkt | or | -jĕkt′ | *n.*
1. A thing that has shape and can be seen or otherwise perceived; a material thing.
2. A thing being viewed, studied, or handled: *Place the object directly beneath the microscope.* **3.** A person or thing toward which an emotion or effort is directed; a target: *an object of ridicule; an object of love.* **4.** A purpose; goal: *the object of the game; his object in requesting a secret meeting.* **5.** In grammar: **a.** A noun, pronoun, noun phrase, or noun clause that receives or is affected by the action of a verb. For example, in the sentence *I sent him a letter, a letter* is the direct object of the verb *sent,* and *him* is the indirect object. **b.** A noun, pronoun, noun phrase, or noun clause that follows a preposition. For example, in *against the tide, the tide* is the object of the preposition *against.*

ob·ject[2] | əb jĕkt′ | *v.* **1.** To express an opposing opinion or argument; protest: *Patrick Henry objected to the British tax on the colonies.* **2.** To be opposed. **3.** To say in opposition or protest: *"Now see here,"* he objected.

72

Challenge Yourself

squad   exotic   apricot   volcanic

Use your Spelling Dictionary to answer these questions. Then write sentences showing that you understand the meaning of each Challenge Word.

1. Would you expect to find a squad of players on a field during a football game?

2. Would you expect to see exotic birds and animals from around the world at a famous zoo?

3. Does an apricot look a lot like a banana?

4. After the fire goes out, would you expect to find volcanic ashes in your fireplace?

Write to the Point

Kim wanted to have a hobby, but she couldn't make up her mind which one to choose. Do you have a hobby? Perhaps you have more than one hobby. Write a paragraph about your favorite hobby or one that you would enjoy. Tell what makes it interesting or fun. Use spelling words from this lesson in your paragraph.

Challenge Use one or more of the Challenge Words in your paragraph.

Proofreading

Use the proofreading marks to show the errors in the paragraph below. Write the five misspelled words correctly in the blanks.

Are modal planes your hobbie Enter this conttest. Win fifty-dollar prize! Fill out the bottum of this page. Then bring your plane the gym by ten o'clok Friday morning.

◯	word is misspelled
∧	word is missing
?∧	question mark is missing

1. _____
2. _____
3. _____
4. _____
5. _____

Lesson 14 Words with /ō/

Listen for /ō/ as you say each word.

almost

comb

ocean

zero

pony

only

total

obey

hotel

motor

program

poem

clothes

coach

oak

coast

soap

throat

toe

goes

1. Which words begin with a vowel and end with a consonant? _____

_____

2. Which words begin with a consonant and end with a vowel? _____

_____

3. Which words begin and end with a vowel? _____

_____

4. Which words begin with the letter p? _____

_____

_____

5. Which word ends with the letter p? _____

6. Which words end with /z/? _____

_____

7. Write the two-syllable words in which the second syllable begins with t.

_____

_____

8. Which word ends with oat? _____

9. Write the words in which you see the letter c but hear /k/. _____

_____

_____

10. Write the word in which you hear /sh/ but don't see the letters sh. _____

11. Write the word in which you see the letter b but don't hear /b/. _____

Checkpoint

Write a spelling word for each clue.
Then use the Checkpoint Study Plan on page 224.

1. I go, you go, he ____.

2. Socks are toes' ____.

3. Not quite means ____.

4. Hand is to finger as foot is to ____.

5. The opposite of disobey is ____.

6. Another word for nothing is ____.

7. One kind of wood is ____.

8. the one and ____

9. as deep as the ____

10. Another word for a TV show is a ____.

11. The person in charge of a team is the ____.

12. Inside your neck is your ____.

13. River is to bank as sea is to ____.

14. A small, full-grown horse is a ____.

15. Suds on a string is rope ____.

16. Another word for sum is ____.

17. A limerick is a kind of ____.

18. brush and ____

19. a place where vacationers stay ____

20. Latin verbs are the roots of many English words. The mystery word and the word <u>move</u> both come from the same root word: *moveo*. <u>Move</u> comes directly from the verb *moveo*. The mystery word comes from another form of the verb *moveo: motus*. Today, the mystery word names a machine that causes things to move. Can you guess it? ____

75

Two Letters

Dear Grandma,

We've been on vacation in Grand Cayman for

_____ a week now. I swim outside

our _____ every day. But the most

exciting thing I've done is to go snorkeling in

the _____.

Leslie decided to take me with her after we'd

been here for _____ one day. She made

me learn the safety rules for swimming under the

water. I had to promise to _____ her!

First, she taught me how to move the funny

rubber feet. Then I learned to breathe through

something that looked like a hose.

Later that afternoon, we went along the

_____ by boat to a coral reef. We

rubbed on something that looked like _____

or cold cream to keep from burning. Also, we

kept our T-shirts on all the time. When we turned

the _____ off and stopped the boat,

Leslie and another diver jumped over the side.

Then I went in yelling, "Here _____ nothing!"

I swam near the surface. I could see all sorts of

brightly colored fish. My feeling was one of

_____ wonder. A silver and black

striped fish swam right in front of me. A canary

fish brushed by my side.

76

Leslie had to drag me out of the water. We looked funny with our _____ sticking to our bodies. So we took a picture, just for you. We didn't even _____ our hair! I got a sore _____, but it was worth it!

Well, that's all for now.

Love,
Tracy

Dear Tracy,

How lucky you are to be on Grand Cayman. The temperature here hit _____ and the old _____ tree is covered with snow. Outside, Mr. Johnson's _____ is puffing his white breath into the air. And here I am, stuck indoors, with this silly broken _____.

I loved your letter. The _____ you wrote on that funny picture was great! Snorkeling really is fun! Before you were born, I filmed a _____ about it right there on Grand Cayman. Of course, that was before I switched to covering baseball!

Well, hurry home! Next week, I get to talk with the _____ of the Cincinnati Reds. Why not join me?

Love you,
Grandma

almost
comb
ocean
zero
pony
only
total
obey
hotel
motor
program
poem
coach
oak
coast
soap
throat
clothes
toe
goes

Capitals

Use a capital letter to begin a person's first or last name. Also, use a capital letter to begin a title that goes with someone's name.

Mrs. Emerick works in the school cafeteria.
Barry and Judy both coach girls' sports.

★ Write the sentences below. Correct the capitalization errors in people's names.

1. laurie, sheila, and karen have passed the rope-climbing drill.

2. miss santucci says that the ropes feel as if they've been waxed with soap.

3. On Tuesday we have a basketball program with mr. dowling.

4. debbie and scott figure out the total number of points that each team scores.

5. marsha, andy, and paul always forget to bring the right clothes for gym.

6. mr. driscoll says we must obey school rules, and so they sit out the game.

7. cindy goes to ballet class almost every Tuesday, so she can't play.

78

Challenge Yourself

appropriate enclosure host foe

Decide which Challenge Word fits each clue. Check your Spelling Dictionary to see if you were right. Then write sentences showing that you understand the meaning of each Challenge Word.

1. This could be used to keep a pet from running away.

2. This word rhymes with <u>ghost</u> and means "a person who entertains guests."

3. An enemy is one of these.

4. If you dress warmly to go out on a very cold day, then your clothing is this.

Write to the Point

Is there a person you like but don't see very often? Write a short letter to this person, telling him or her some of the news in your life. You might want to share a special event, something funny, or some of your plans for the future. Use spelling words from this lesson in your letter.

Challenge Use one or more of the Challenge Words in your letter.

Proofreading

Use the proofreading marks to show the errors in the paragraph below. Write the five misspelled words correctly in the blanks.

Almost every day Mr kane gos to the beach for a swim Sometimes i go with him. I wear a swimsuit under my cloze, but I usually stick onely one tow in the chilly oshun.

⬭	word is misspelled
⊙	period is missing
≡	letter should be capitalized

1. _____

2. _____

3. _____

4. _____

5. _____

Lesson 15 Words with /ō/

Listen for /ō/ as you say each word.

nose

froze

chose

close

those

broke

alone

explode

stole

knows

slowly

below

shadow

hollow

tomorrow

own

window

elbow

pillow

though

1. Write the words that end with /z/.

_____ _____

_____ _____

_____ _____

2. Write the words that begin with the letter s and have two syllables. _____

_____

3. Which words begin with the letter b?

_____

4. Which words begin with a vowel?

_____ _____

_____ _____

5. Write the words that are spelled with a double consonant. ll _____

ll _____   rr _____

6. Which word ends with the same four letters as dough? _____

7. Which word ends with the same three letters as hole? _____

8. Which words end with the same three letters as widow? _____

_____

9. Write the word in which you see the letter k but don't hear /k/. _____

10. Which words have three vowel letters but two vowel sounds? _____

_____

Checkpoint

Write a spelling word for each clue.
Then use the Checkpoint Study Plan on page 224.

1. Drums make sounds because they are ___.
2. took something belonging to another ___
3. Another word for understands is ___.
4. not quickly, but ___
5. To have means to ___.
6. Today I freeze, yesterday I ___.
7. not these, but ___
8. Leg is to knee as arm is to ___.
9. A red center of the face is a rose ___.
10. Sunshine casts a ___.
11. Another word for however is ___.
12. as soft as a feather ___
13. The opposite of far is ___.
14. Cannons and firecrackers do this. ___
15. yesterday, today, and ___
16. The opposite of above is ___.
17. Without company means ___.
18. The glass vase fell and ___.
19. Another word for picked is ___.

20. This mystery word comes from the old Viking word *vindauga*. A *vindauga* was an opening in the wall of a house. *Vindauga* meant wind-eye. This is because a *vindauga* was an opening (or eye) through which the wind might enter the house. The mystery word is the name for an opening in a wall. Today this opening is covered with glass. Guess the mystery word. ___

POP'S OLD BARN

Use each word once to complete this story.

The old barn on the Wilson farm stood on the hilltop. Its frame cast a _____ in the moonlight and looked like a _____ face as light came through the _____ frames. People said that it was haunted. Young John Wilson agreed.

"Count me out, if you're going to Pop's old barn," John told his friends.

"I don't think that place is scary," Mike said. "Do you, Lee?"

Lee answered, "No, I don't."

"Let's search the barn _____ night. Who's going with me?" asked Mike.

Lee spoke up. "I will."

But John said, "I wish my pop would tear it down. Count me out."

Late the next evening, Mike and Lee quietly _____ through the Wilson land to the barn. _____, they removed a wooden bolt from the door. The squeaking noise made their skin crawl. Standing _____ together, they tiptoed through the pitch-black room. Then suddenly, Mike felt something brush past him. He _____ in his place.

"What was that?" he whispered.

"Silly, it's just a mouse!" Lee laughed. Then she looked around. "Let's go home!" she begged. "Who _____ what's inside this place!"

"No, let's go on," Mike said. He grabbed Lee by the _____ and led her to the ladder just _____ the loft.

As they began to climb, they heard a "crack." A rung of the ladder _____ beneath Mike's foot, sending him falling to the ground.

"Look!" shouted Mike.

A strange, purple light was circling the room. The light stopped before a pale, white face and a wild laugh filled the barn.

"Help!" Lee screamed. Then she ran like a scared rabbit.

"Hey, Lee, don't leave me _____!" Mike's voice seemed to _____ from inside him. He shot out the door!

Inside his family's _____ barn, John laughed and laughed. He tossed off the case from his mom's old _____. He had cut holes for his eyes and _____. He circled his purple flashlight once more around the room.

Then he walked down the ladder, out the door, and away from his favorite hideout . . . Pop's old barn.

- The children _____ to explore the old barn.
- They were frightened even _____ they didn't believe in ghosts.
- John couldn't believe that they fell for _____ silly tricks!

83

nose
froze
chose
close
those
broke
alone
explode
stole
knows
slowly
below
shadow
hollow
tomorrow
own
window
elbow
pillow
though

Quotation Marks

Place quotation marks around the exact words of a speaker. Notice the position of the quotation marks and commas:

> *Robin groaned, "I'm going to the dentist tomorrow."*
> *Albert asked, "Are you going alone?"*

★ The end punctuation comes inside the final quotation marks. Rewrite the following sentences, adding quotation marks and other punctuation.

1. Bob said That window must be replaced

_____

2. Randy asked Is this pillow made of feathers

_____

3. Jim said My cast goes up to my elbow

_____

Sometimes a speaker's exact words are at the beginning of a sentence. The quotation marks are placed around the exact words of the speaker, but notice the position of the punctuation marks.

> *"Did you hear the fireworks explode?" asked Ron.*
> *"Those fireworks are really beautiful," said Julie.*

★ Rewrite the following sentences with correct punctuation.

4. What can we do with that hollow log asked Christine

_____

_____

5. Let's keep close together during the hike said the guide

_____

_____

6. Look at your shadow on the wall yelled Michael

WORDS AT WORK

Challenge Yourself

bouquet   dispose   stow   sow

What do you think each underlined Challenge Word means? Check your Spelling Dictionary to see if you are right. Then write sentences showing that you understand the meaning of each Challenge Word.

1. The flowers were made into a beautiful <u>bouquet</u>.

2. Please use the garbage can to <u>dispose</u> of any trash.

3. Passengers must <u>stow</u> their suitcases under their seats or in a closet.

4. In spring we <u>sow</u> grass seed on our front lawn.

Write to the Point

The story "Pop's Old Barn" contains some exact details that describe the barn. Write a paragraph describing a place that you know well. It may be your room, an attic, or a place outdoors. Include details that tell what you see, hear, and feel when you are there. Use spelling words from this lesson in your description.

Challenge Use one or more of the Challenge Words in your description.

Proofreading

Use the proofreading marks to show the errors in the paragraph below. Write the five misspelled words correctly in the blanks.

Mario was alone in his room at night. Suddenly he frose. Did something move near the windoe Mario felt as as thogh his heart would expload. Then he had to laugh. It is was his own shaddow.

⭕	word is misspelled
✗	take out word
?	question mark is missing

1. _____

2. _____

3. _____

4. _____

5. _____

85

Lesson 16 Words with /ŭ/

Listen for /ŭ/ as you say each word.

brush
until
under
jungle
fudge
button
subject
hundred
knuckle
suddenly
hunt

double
trouble
enough
rough
tough
country
touch
couple

does

1. Write the words that end with /f/.

_____

_____

2. Write the words that end with the letters ble.

_____

3. Write the one-syllable words that begin with the letter t. _____

_____

4. Which word begins with /j/? _____

5. Which word ends with /j/? _____

6. Which words begin with a vowel?

_____

_____

7. Write the two-syllable words that begin and end with a consonant. _____

_____

8. Write the word that begins with /n/.

_____

9. Write the word in which you see the letter s but hear /z/. _____

10. Which word ends with the same three letters as slush? _____

11. Which word ends with the same three letters as bunt? _____

12. Which word has three syllables?

_____

13. Which words begin with the letter c?

_____

Checkpoint

Write a spelling word for each clue.
Then use the Checkpoint Study Plan on page 224.

1. comb and ___

2. Leg is to knee as finger is to ___.

3. "It happened all at once!" Tom said ___.

4. I do, you do, he ___.

5. Ninety-nine plus one equals one ___.

6. The opposite of over is ___.

7. Another word for search is ___.

8. Math is a school ___.

9. Foxes are to forest as jaguars are to ___.

10. When you have problems, you are in ___.

11. Skyscraper is to city as barn is to ___.

12. Up to the time of means ___.

13. not too much—just ___

14. To compare candy is to judge ___.

15. not smooth, but ___

16. Twice means ___.

17. Chewy meat is probably ___.

18. To feel is to ___.

19. Two people are a ___.

20. The French word for a flower bud is *bouton*.
The word *bouton* has given us our mystery
word. The mystery word names a little knob
that keeps a shirt, dress, or coat closed. This
knob pushes out through its hole like a flower
bud pushes out through its leaves. So the
French called this knob a *bud* or *bouton*. Can
you guess the mystery word? ___

The Oral Report

Danny was scared. He stared at the clock in Mr. Oliverio's room. Only 20 minutes _____ recess! By then all this would be over.

"Maybe he'll forget," Danny wished. "I'll bet there isn't _____ time to hear everyone today, anyway."

Danny started to _____ through his desk for his notes. Mr. Oliverio began, "The _____ of this week's geography lesson is the _____ along the Amazon River. We are going to hear several reports from our South America committee. _____ the group have everything in order?"

"Yes, Mr. Oliverio," said Steve White.

"Steve's a _____ kid," Danny thought. "He can handle this."

Danny felt Steve _____ past him as he stepped to the front of the room. He was surprised to see Steve's hands shaking. Poor Steve was holding his notes so tightly that each _____ on his hands was white!

"BRAZIL," he began. "Brazil is the largest _____ in South America. Its population is more than _____ that of other South American countries. . . ."

Danny barely heard Steve's speech as he played with a loose _____ on his shirt. He thought about the _____ cake that he would eat at recess. Danny looked at the clock again. In a _____ of minutes, the bell would ring.

"Very nice, Steven. And now, we will hear from Daniel about the Amazon River."

Danny's heart pounded! His shaking, wet hands reached _____ his desk for the map he had made for the report.

"Oh, no," he thought. "I guess I'm in _____ now! Where's my map?"

_____, he felt his fingers _____ the map. Danny stepped to the front of the room.

"The Amazon River begins in the Andes Mountains and flows eastward through Brazil," he shouted. "More than two _____ small rivers flow into the Amazon. . . ."

Before he knew it, the speech was done and the recess bell rang. Steve ran up to Danny.

"That wasn't as _____ as I had thought it would be!"

Then Michelle Farrell joined them. "Hey, guys. You were great! Were you scared?"

"Are you kidding?" laughed Danny. "It was nothing!"

brush
until
under
jungle
fudge
button
subject
hundred
knuckle
suddenly
hunt
double
trouble
enough
rough
tough
country
touch
couple
does

Pronunciation

A dictionary lists a pronunciation for each entry word. This pronunciation is written in special symbols. The symbols are a guide to the sounds of a word and are called the **sound spelling**.

> **pro·nun·ci·a·tion** | prə nŭn′sē ā′shən | *n.* **1.** The act or manner of pronouncing words. **2.** A phonetic representation of a word, showing how it is pronounced. **—modifier:** *a pronunciation key.*

★ Put the following group of words in alphabetical order. Then look up each word in the Spelling Dictionary and write the sound spelling beside each word.

hundred   couple   rough   touch

1. _____   _____

2. _____   _____

3. _____   _____

4. _____   _____

★ The words below are followed by two sound spellings, one correct and one incorrect. Look up each word in the Spelling Dictionary. Write each word and its correct sound spelling.

5. does   /dăs/   /dŭz/   _____

6. button   **/bŭt′ n/**   **/bŏt′ ŏn/**   _____

7. fudge   /fŭj/   /fŭdj/   _____

8. under   /ŭn′ dər/   /ūn′ dər/   _____

★ Which spelling words do these sound spellings represent? Write each word and copy its sound spelling. Check your answers in the Spelling Dictionary.

9. /tŭf/   _____

10. **/nŭk′əl/**   _____

11. **/kŭn′trē/**   _____

12. /ĭ nŭf′/   _____

13. /hŭnt/

Challenge Yourself

customary   countryside
       erupt   construct

Use your Spelling Dictionary to answer these questions. Then write sentences showing that you understand the meaning of each Challenge Word.

1. Is it <u>customary</u> for students to study for tests at a party?

2. Would a book about volcanoes probably tell why they <u>erupt</u>?

3. Would it be wise to <u>construct</u> a boat out of paper?

4. Would the <u>countryside</u> be a good place to find insects and wildflowers?

Write to the Point

Like Danny, most people feel nervous before they give an oral report. Have you given an oral report? What advice would you give Danny to help him make sure that his talk goes smoothly? Write a list of things he could do before and during his speech. Use spelling words from this lesson in your list.

Challenge Use one or more of the Challenge Words in your list.

Proofreading

Use the proofreading marks to show the errors in the paragraph below. Write the five misspelled words correctly in the blanks.

>   I had untill Friday to do a ruff copy my oral report on Martin Luther King, Jr I had no trubble finding enogh facts on my subject, since Dr King was a great leader in this contry.

⬭	word is misspelled
⊙	period is missing
∧	word is missing

1. _____

2. _____

3. _____

4. _____

5. _____

Lesson 17 Contractions

Say each word.

don't

doesn't

didn't

isn't

hadn't

wasn't

weren't

aren't

haven't

couldn't

wouldn't

shouldn't

I'm

you'd

she'd

they'll

they've

we're

let's

that's

Solve these contraction puzzles.

has + not = <u>hasn't</u>

1. do + not = _____

2. is + not = _____

3. are + not = _____

4. did + not = _____

5. was + not = _____

6. had + not = _____

7. does + not = _____

8. were + not = _____

9. have + not = _____

10. could + not = _____

11. would + not = _____

12. should + not = _____

13. you + had = _____

14. she + had = _____

15. they + have = _____

16. they + will = _____

17. we + are = _____

18. let + us = _____

19. that + is = _____

20. I + am = _____

Checkpoint

Write a spelling word for each clue.
Then use the Checkpoint Study Plan on page 224.

1. The opposite of is is ___.

2. Ought not means ___.

3. I thought they were home but they ___.

4. It isn't, they ___

5. The opposite of would is ___.

6. Babies often hear this from parents. ___

7. Do not have means ___.

8. I thought I could drive but I really ___.

9. The opposite of does is ___.

10. I did my homework but my friend ___.

11. The opposite of had is ___.

12. The opposite of was is ___.

Write the contractions that take the place of the underlined words.

13. That is my house on the corner. ___

14. Mom and I are going on a bike trip. ___

15. Beth, Tim, and Ron will speak today. ___

16. You had better be careful! ___

17. I am going to visit my cousin. ___

18. Janice would like that new album. ___

19. Let us see about cleaning up our school. ___

20. Bob, Ted, and Ann have gone to the lake. ___

PECOS BILL

There _____ many coyotes who can remember the days when Pecos Bill grew up. It _____ every day that a boy grows up with coyotes. But then, Pecos Bill _____ an everyday fellow.

As a baby, Bill drank mountain lions' milk. Now _____ think that this would be hard to get! But for Bill's mother, it was a snap. Why, _____ fight off an army, single-handed.

Pecos Bill's father was one of the first to settle Texas, back when there _____ many people around. But when people started settling just 50 miles away, he knew it was time to go!

"This country's too crowded," he would say. "_____ pack up our things. _____ moving farther west."

So they piled into a wagon, with baby Bill in the back. As they crossed the Pecos River, there was a bump that sent Bill flying! He _____ call out for help.

But in all the excitement of moving, Bill's family
_____ notice he was gone until four
weeks later. Then his dad said, "Some people will
find him. _____ take care of him."

Bill was taken in by a pack of coyotes. For ten
happy years, Bill lived among them. Since he
_____ seen any people, Bill was sure
that he was one of the pack.

One day, a cowboy came riding along and
spotted Bill fighting a bear. The cowboy promised
that he _____ hurt Bill, but of
course, Bill couldn't understand. The cowboy taught
Bill to speak. He told Bill that he was a boy.

"But _____ a coyote!" Bill said. "Listen, I can
howl. Ah-ooooo!"

"That _____ mean a thing!" said
the cowboy, tossing Bill a shirt. "Real coyotes
have big fur coats, _____ they? Look at
them. _____ all got fur."

Bill glanced around. "I _____ got
any fur."

"You _____ be living out
here. _____ for sure," said the cowboy.
"Come home with me."

So Bill said good-by to his animal family.

"I'll never forget you," he said, in coyote talk.

And Pecos Bill climbed upon his pet mountain
lion and galloped off to a new life as the best
cowboy the Texas prairie has ever seen.

don't
doesn't
didn't
isn't
hadn't
wasn't
weren't
aren't
haven't
couldn't
wouldn't
shouldn't
I'm
you'd
she'd
they'll
they've
we're
let's
that's

Contractions

A contraction combines two words into one word by leaving out one or more letters. An apostrophe shows where the letters have been left out.

is not = isn't   she would = she'd

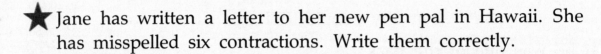

 Jane has written a letter to her new pen pal in Hawaii. She has misspelled six contractions. Write them correctly.

> *Dear Leah,*
>
> *Ia'm a fourth grader in Santa Fe, New Mexico. Wer're in the same grade, aern't we? My family lives in the city of Santa Fe, but it isnn't far to drive into the country. The land is very dry here. Plants doen't grow easily. But I think New Mexico is beautiful, and I wouldnt want to live anyplace else.*
>
> *Hawaii must be beautiful, too. I've seen lots of pictures of people surfing. Do you surf? Please write.*
>
> *Jane Trout*

1. _____   2. _____   3. _____

4. _____   5. _____   6. _____

 Leah wrote this letter back to Jane. She has misspelled four contractions. Find the words and write them correctly.

> *Dear Jane,*
>
> *Lett's be pen pals. I'd like to know more about you.*
>
> *I live on the island of Kauai. Yod'd really like Kauai. It has beautiful waterfalls. Trees and plants grow everywhere.*
>
> *Yes, I go surfing. If I culdnnt, I don't know what I would do! I told my family that I am writing to you. Theyve' said that you should come to visit.*
>
> *Leah Suzaki*

7. _____   8. _____

9. _____   10. _____

96

Challenge Yourself

___

it'd   should've   must've   there're

___

Write the two words that you think make up each underlined Challenge Word. Check your Spelling Dictionary to see if you were right. Then write sentences using each Challenge Word correctly.

1. There're some great storytellers in my family.

3. My grandfather should've written his stories down to help me remember them.

2. I must've been three years old when I first heard the story about the pet crocodile.

4. The story isn't true, but it'd make a great movie.

Write to the Point

Write a short tall tale of your own about a superhero like Pecos Bill. What amazing powers does your hero have? Is your hero very strong, very brave, very smart? How does he or she use these powers? Remember that tall tales stretch the truth, so let your imagination go. Use spelling words from this lesson in your tall tale.

Challenge Use one or more of the Challenge Words in your tall tale.

Proofreading

Use the proofreading marks to show the errors in the paragraph below. Write the five misspelled words correctly in the blanks.

> word is misspelled
>
> ⊙ period is missing
>
> ═ letter should be capitalized

If I had'nd seen it, i wuldn't have believed it. the man couldnt have been less than ten feet tall Lets just say he wasunt the type you'd expect to see in my town.

1. _____

2. _____

3. _____

4. _____

5. _____

Lesson 18 Words in Review

A. swallow
solve
hospital
problem
hobby
knock

B. poem
obey
throat
goes
motor

C. froze
shadow
tomorrow
though

D. subject
double
trouble
does
suddenly

★Use a piece of paper for the starred activities.

1. In Lesson 13 you studied two ways to spell /ŏ/: o, a. Write the words in list A.

_____   _____

_____   _____

_____   _____

2. In Lesson 14 you studied three ways to spell /ō/: o, oa, oe. Write the words in list B.

_____   _____

_____   _____

_____   _____

★**3.** Write the words in lists A and B. Look up each word in the Spelling Dictionary and write the part of speech beside each word. (Hint: Some words may be more than one part of speech.)

4. In Lesson 15 you studied three ways to spell /ō/: o—e, ow, ou. Write the words in list C.

_____   _____

_____   _____

5. In Lesson 16 you studied three ways to spell /ŭ/: u, ou, oe. Write the words in list D.

_____   _____

_____   _____

_____   _____

★**6.** Now write a sentence for each review word in lists C and D.

★**7.** Write all review words in alphabetical order.

★**8.** Divide the review words you wrote into syllables.

98

Writer's Workshop

A Friendly Letter

Writing a letter is a good way to keep in touch with someone. In a friendly letter, you can write in the same way that you speak. You might share some news about yourself or someone you know. You might also tell your thoughts or feelings about a subject or event. Here is part of a letter that Judy wrote to her grandmother.

> **Dear Grandma,**
>
> **You won't believe this! Tabitha had seven kittens. Four are gray, two are black, and one is striped. Mom won't let us keep any of them, and it's going to be really sad giving them away. Oh, well. At least we've found good homes for them. I guess even one more cat would be too much for this apartment.**

To write her letter, Judy followed the steps in the writing process. She began with a **Prewriting** activity using a list. In her list she wrote several things that she might include in her letter. Her list helped her decide what to tell her grandmother. Part of Judy's list is shown here. Study what Judy did. Which details about the kittens did she use in her letter?

Letter to Grandma

Tabitha's kittens
    seven!
    they are all asleep right now
    have to give away
    found good homes

two new friends
like to skate
in my class

Get ready to write your own friendly letter. Write to a friend or family member you haven't seen in a while. Before you begin, make a list of the news in your life. Choose the news you think will interest your reader. Then follow the other steps in the writing process—**Writing, Revising, Proofreading,** and **Publishing.**

Lesson 19 Words with /ŭ/

Listen for /ŭ/ as you say each word.

won
wonderful
month
front
among
other
brother
another
cover
discover
money
monkey
done
sponge
nothing
above
stomach
once
become

blood

1. Which words have one syllable and end with a consonant? _____

_____ _____

_____

2. Which words have one syllable and end with a vowel? _____

_____ _____

3. Which words end with the letters er?

_____ _____

_____ _____

_____

4. Write the two-syllable words that begin with a vowel. _____

_____ _____

5. In which words is /ē/ spelled with the letters ey?

_____ _____

6. Write the words in which you see three vowel letters but hear only two vowel sounds.

_____ _____

7. Write the word in which you see the letters ch but hear /k/. _____

8. Write the word in which you hear /w/ but don't see the letter w. _____

9. Write the word that begins with the letter w and has three syllables. _____

10. Write the compound words.

_____ _____

Checkpoint

Write a spelling word for each clue.
Then use the Checkpoint Study Plan on page 224.

1. Thirst is to throat as hunger is to ____.

2. The opposite of something is ____.

3. You must choose one or ____.

4. not twice, but ____

5. Yesterday I became, today I will ____.

6. Today I win, yesterday I ____.

7. Along with means ____.

8. An absorbing object is a ____.

9. terrific, fantastic, and ____

10. Tree is to sap as human body is to ____.

11. The opposite of back is ____.

12. dollars and cents ____

13. sister and ____

14. not below, but ____

15. One-twelfth of a year is a ____.

16. What's finished is ____.

17. I don't want this. I want the ____.

18. A baboon is a kind of ____.

19-20. A prefix is one or more letters added to the beginning of a word. It changes the meaning of the word it is added to and makes a new word. The first mystery word means to remove from view. The second mystery word is formed by adding the prefix <u>dis</u> to the first mystery word. This gives it the <u>opposite</u> meaning. The second word means to bring into view or find out. Can you guess the mystery words? ____ ____

101

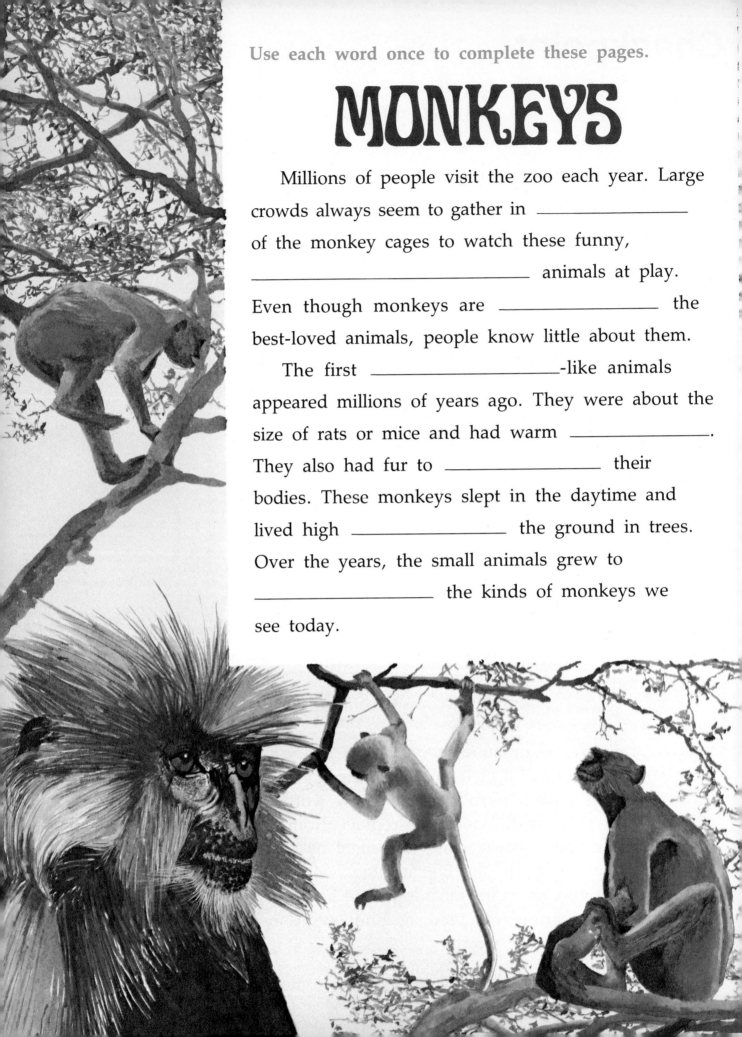

MONKEYS

Millions of people visit the zoo each year. Large crowds always seem to gather in _____ of the monkey cages to watch these funny, _____ animals at play. Even though monkeys are _____ the best-loved animals, people know little about them.

The first _____-like animals appeared millions of years ago. They were about the size of rats or mice and had warm _____. They also had fur to _____ their bodies. These monkeys slept in the daytime and lived high _____ the ground in trees. Over the years, the small animals grew to _____ the kinds of monkeys we see today.

Most monkeys live in places that are warm every
_____ of the year. There must be trees
and plenty of food! A large monkey may need more
than 50 bananas to fill its _____!

Monkeys live in groups. Sometimes the group is
divided into families. There can be a father, a
mother, and even a _____ and
sister in a family! Monkeys watch out for one
_____. If one animal should
_____ danger, it will call
an alarm for the _____ monkeys.

Monkeys are very smart. They can make and use
tools. Some people have seen them using dried-up
leaves as a _____ to soak up water;
others have seen them using sticks to dig. Monkeys
have even been used in space flights! Some
scientists have _____ awards for the work
done with these monkeys.

Each year the number of monkeys grows smaller.
One reason is that the _____-great jungles
of the world are being cut down. Also, some
monkeys are killed for their fur, which is worth a
lot of _____.

What is being _____ to stop the killing
of monkeys? Laws to protect them have often
been helpful.

Many people feel that it would be wrong to
do _____. What do you think?

won
wonderful
month
front
among
other
brother
another
cover
discover
money
monkey
done
sponge
nothing
above
stomach
once
become
blood

Accent Marks

The sound spellings in a dictionary tell how to pronounce a word. An accent mark (') is a part of this guide. It tells which syllable in a word is spoken with more stress or force.

⭐ The sound spellings for four words are printed below. Look at where the accent marks are placed in each word. Then answer the questions that follow.

among	/ə **mŭng′**/	cover	/**kŭv′** ər/
become	/bĭ **kŭm′**/	monkey	/**mŭng′** kē/

1. Write the words that have the accent on the first syllable.

   _____   _____

2. Write the words that have the accent on the second syllable.

   _____   _____

⭐ Decide which sound spelling stands for a spelling word. Then write the word and its correct sound spelling.

3. /**mŭn′** ē/   /mŭn **ē′**/   _____

4. /nŭth **ĭng′**/   /**nŭth′** ĭng/   _____

5. /**ə′** bŭv/   /ə **bŭv′**/   _____

6. /**brŭth′** ər/   /brŭth **ər′**/   _____

Some words of two or more syllables have two accented syllables. The strongest accent is called the **primary accent:** ('). The weaker accent is called the **secondary accent:** (').

⭐ Look at the sound spelling for this word: /**yĕs′**tər dā′/

7. Which syllable has the primary accent? _____

8. Which syllable has the secondary accent? _____

9. Write the word <u>yesterday</u>. _____

WORDS AT WORK

Challenge Yourself

loveliest   hover
   wondrous   undiscovered

What do you think each underlined Challenge Word means? Check your Spelling Dictionary to see if you are right. Then write sentences showing that you understand the meaning of each Challenge Word.

1. The beautiful tulips made Ping's garden the <u>loveliest</u> one in town.

2. We watched the hummingbird <u>hover</u> near the flowers.

3. Visiting the museum was a <u>wondrous</u> experience for Anita.

4. Although we know a great deal about our oceans, many of their secrets remain <u>undiscovered</u>.

Write to the Point

What kinds of animals have you seen in your everyday life? Have you observed animals such as dogs, cats, fish, birds, insects, squirrels, or rabbits? Choose an animal and write a short report. What does it eat? How does it sleep and play? How does it act around other animals? Use spelling words from this lesson in your report.

Challenge Use one or more of the Challenge Words in your report.

Proofreading

Use the proofreading marks to show the errors in the paragraph below. Write the five misspelled words correctly in the blanks.

⬭	word is misspelled
↵	take out word
? ∧	question mark is missing

My bruther Dan he has become a bird watcher. He wonce saw an an owl in our front yard. Anuther time he saw a robin amung the bushes. What else will he discuver

1. _____

2. _____

3. _____

4. _____

5. _____

Lesson 20 Words with /o͝o/

Listen for /o͝o/ as you say each word.

understood
notebook
wool
brook
cooked
wooden
stood
good-by

full
pudding
bush
sugar
pull
during

could
would
should
yours

woman
wolf

1. Which words end with /d/?

   _____ _____

   _____

2. Which word begins with the letter d?

   _____

3. Which word ends with /z/? _____

4. Write the words that contain double consonants.

   ll _____ ll _____

   dd _____

5. Which word ends with the same three letters as push? _____

6. Which words end with the same three letters as cook? _____

   _____

7. Write the word in which you hear /sh/ but do not see the letters sh. _____

8. Write the word in which you see the letters ed but hear /t/. _____

9. Write the compound words. Circle the word that is connected by a hyphen. _____

   _____

10. Write the words that begin with the letter w.

   _____ _____

   _____ _____

Checkpoint

Write a spelling word for each clue.
Then use the Checkpoint Study Plan on page 224.

1. A little river may be a babbling ___.

2. The opposite of push is ___.

3. Ought to means ___.

4. not mine, but ___

5. as sweet as ___

6. A girl grows up to be a ___.

7. Sheep's clothing is ___.

8. Today I will, yesterday I ___.

9. Things that are made of wood are ___.

10. Where the trees were is where the woods ___.

11. A creamy dessert is chocolate ___.

12. The opposite of raw is ___.

13. Was able to means ___.

14. Another word for shrub is ___.

15. Another word for writing pad is ___.

16. not before, not after, but ___

17. a dog-like animal ___

18. What's known is ___.

19. The opposite of empty is ___.

20. This mystery word is what we say when we wish someone farewell. It comes from the phrase "God be with you." This phrase was shortened to "God be wy you." Then it was further shortened to "Godbwye." Can you guess what the mystery word was finally shortened to? ___

107

Use each word once to complete these pages.

The Widow Novik's Place

An old _____ bridge crossed a _____ on the edge of town. Just past the bridge _____ a lonely cabin. When the first autumn breeze blew, my sister, Caroline, and I would _____ on our _____ sweaters and head down to the Widow Novik's.

We _____ walk through the woods and swamps, sometimes spotting a deer hiding behind a _____. Once, late at night, we heard a _____ howling! Our visits to the Widow Novik meant a lot to us. And we knew that they meant a lot to her, too.

Most people thought that the Widow was a strange old _____. They said that their children _____ stay away from her cabin. But whenever the Widow's name came up at Town Meeting, Ma and Pa would take her side. Of course, the neighbors _____ never understand this, but Caroline and I surely _____! Especially after our visit in October, 1892.

Caroline brought the Widow some of her needlework. I brought some _____ cookies that Ma had baked. The Widow served us each a bowl _____ of delicious chocolate _____. She _____ the best in the county. Then, I read the Widow a story that I had written about her.

"Wait, Jonathan," she said. "I want to give you something. . . . My diary," she went on, handing me an old _____. "Take it. It's _____."

And from its pages, I read about her hard times _____ the Civil War. As I closed the book, a letter fell out:

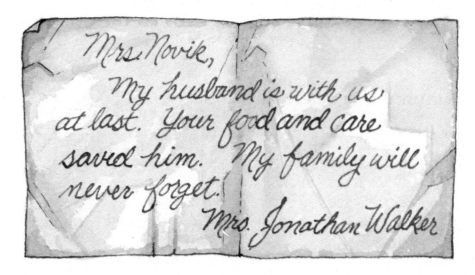

Mrs. Novik,
My husband is with us at last. Your food and care saved him. My family will never forget.
Mrs. Jonathan Walker

"Mrs. Jonathan Walker? Grandma!" All at once I knew why the Widow Novik was so important to us. I remembered Grandma's stories about the people of the Underground Railroad and the lady who hid runaway slaves during the war. Now I knew that the lady who hid Grandpa was the Widow Novik.

Soon, we said, "_____!" until next time.

The cabin is gone now; so is that old bridge. But sometimes, even now, I like to think about that autumn day at the Widow Novik's place.

understood
notebook
wool
brook
cooked
wooden
stood
good-by
full
pudding
bush
sugar
pull
during
could
would
should
yours
woman
wolf

Capitals

When the words <u>mother</u>, <u>father</u>, <u>mom</u>, and <u>dad</u> are used in place of names, they begin with a capital letter. These words do not begin with a capital letter when they follow a possessive word such as <u>my</u>, <u>your</u>, or <u>Bob's</u>.

We bought Mother a new plant.
My dad gave my mom a new dress.

★ Correct the errors in these sentences:

1. A wuman called mom with an important message.

_____

_____

2. My Father stoud in line for baseball tickets.

_____

3. Danny's Dad bought a bucket of cookt chicken.

_____

4. We took a picture of mom and dad near the wuden bridge.

_____

_____

When words like <u>aunt</u>, <u>uncle</u>, and <u>doctor</u> are used as titles before a name, they begin with a capital letter. They do not begin with a capital letter when they are used without a name.

★ Correct the errors in these sentences:

5. The chocolate puding was made by uncle Sam.

_____

6. aunt Sally makes the best suger cookies.

_____

7. My uncle helped dad pul our car out of the snow.

_____

Challenge Yourself

bookstore   misunderstood
     rural   swoosh

Decide which Challenge Word fits each clue. Check your Spelling Dictionary to see if you were right. Then write sentences showing that you understand the meaning of each Challenge Word.

1. This is an area where there are farms and much open land.

2. This is the sound that your snow skis would make if you were racing down a mountain.

3. A writer does <u>not</u> want to be this.

4. This is a building that may have only one floor but a great many stories.

Write to the Point

The Widow Novik was an important person to Jonathan and his family in the story. Is there an older person in your family or in your neighborhood who is interesting or important to you? Write a paragraph that describes this person. Include the details that make this person special. Use spelling words from this lesson in your paragraph.

Challenge Use one or more of the Challenge Words in your paragraph.

Proofreading

Use the proofreading marks to show the errors in the paragraph below. Write the five misspelled words correctly in the blanks.

◯	word is misspelled
≡	letter should be capitalized
∧	word is missing

Durring the late 1800s, Mrs. Lee was a young women. Her life very different from yurs. she fished in a brook. She also made maple suger from sap spun yarn from wull.

1. _____
2. _____
3. _____
4. _____
5. _____

111

Lesson 21 /ōō/ and /yōō/

Listen for /ōō/ or /yōō/ as you say each word.

shoot

choose

goose

loose

cartoon

balloon

too

soup

group

cougar

route

through

new

knew

grew

truly

truth

fruit

two

beautiful

1. Which words end with /t/? _____

_____

2. Which words end with the letter p? _____

_____

3. Which word ends with /z/? _____

4. Which words end with /s/? _____

_____

5. Which words begin with /k/? _____

6. Write the word in which you see the letter k but don't hear /k/. _____

7. Which words begin with the letter t and end with a vowel? _____

_____

8. Which word begins with the letters thr? _____

9. Which word contains a double consonant? _____

10. Which word has three syllables? _____

11. Which words have the same spelling of /ōō/ as blew? _____

_____

12. Which word begins like trick and ends with the letters uth? _____

13. In which word is /ōō/ spelled with the letters ui? _____

Checkpoint

Write a spelling word for each clue.
Then use the Checkpoint Study Plan on page 224.

1. You can do this with a camera or a gun. ——
2. not alone, but in a ——
3. To pass between is to go ——.
4. Got bigger means ——.
5. It's full of hot air—it's a ——.
6. If I understood, then I ——.
7. Potato is to vegetable as banana is to ——.
8. Eat and spell with alphabet ——.
9. What's good for the gander is good for the ——.
10. Saturday morning television has at least one ——.
11. The opposite of tight is ——.
12. Another word for pretty is ——.
13. One plus one is ——.
14. a way to get there ——
15. as good as ——
16. Another word for pick is ——.
17. The opposite of falsehood is ——.
18. "I never tell a lie," Tom said ——.
19. Also means ——.

20. This mystery word names an animal. The word
    comes from the Tupi Indian word *suasuarana*.
    Suasuarana means false deer. They chose this
    name because the animal is colored like a deer.
    The name became *cuguacuarana* in New Latin.
    Then it became *couguar* in French. What do you
    think we call this animal in English? ——

Use each word once to complete these pages.

THE COUGAR

The mountain lion, or _____, is a _____ wonderful animal. It once lived in every part of the United States. Today, it is the sad _____ that this strong and _____ animal is hardly ever seen.

Mountain lions have as many as five cubs at a time. The cubs live together in a _____ with their mother for about _____ years. She teaches them how to hunt. Then she turns them _____ to hunt on their own. When mountain lions hunt for deer, they follow the deer _____ the forest. They look for an old or sick deer. Then they _____ one to kill for food. If there are no mountain lions, the deer herds get _____ big. Then all the deer starve because there is not enough food for so many of them.

People used to _____ mountain lions. They thought they were bad. If they _____ what we know about these helpful animals they would have let them live. Now we are trying to put mountain lions back in places where deer herds are getting too big. Most of them seem to like their _____ homes.

The Ballad of a Wildlife Photographer

Jane took off in a hot-air _____,

On a cool summer night late in June.

Some pictures to shoot,

Along this air _____,

Her brother would draw a _____.

Now her brother was called "Little Dan."

He liked vegetable _____ in a can.

But they had only _____,

Along this air route,

And a package of Moo-Goo-Gai-Pan.

"I'm homesick," he started to boom.

"And I feel like I'm trapped in a tomb!

I miss my pet _____,

The one Mom let loose,

How I wish I were in my own room!"

Well, Jane's trip _____ annoying and long.

Since everything started off wrong.

But her snapshots were great,

And Dan really can't wait,

Till the next time she takes him along.

shoot
choose
goose
loose
cartoon
balloon
too
soup
group
cougar
route
new
knew
grew
truly
truth
fruit
through
two
beautiful

Homophones

Words that sound alike but have different spellings and meanings are called **homophones**. If a word is a homophone, a dictionary will list the other homophone at the end of the entry.

The wind blew the blue balloon into the trees.

★ Find the words <u>route</u> and <u>root</u> in the Spelling Dictionary. Then write their sound spellings and definitions.

1. route _____

2. root _____

★ Write the correct word, <u>route</u> or <u>root</u>, in each sentence below.

3. I took the shortest _____ to school.
4. The _____ of the plant helps to feed it.

★ Use the Spelling Dictionary to check the meanings of these homophones:

knew   new   too   two   to

5. Which word is the opposite of <u>old</u>? _____
6. Which word is the past tense of <u>know</u>? _____
7. Which word equals one plus one? _____
8. Which word means <u>also</u>? _____

★ Read all the definitions of <u>through</u> and <u>threw</u> in the Spelling Dictionary. Then correct any spelling errors in these sentences.

9. The quarterback through the ball into the end zone.

10. The hikers walked threw the forest.

116

Challenge Yourself

accuse boost contribute coupon

Use your Spelling Dictionary to answer these questions. Then write sentences showing that you understand the meaning of each Challenge Word.

1. Would a small child need a <u>boost</u> to climb up a tree?

2. Do you pay more money for an item at the grocery store when you use a <u>coupon</u>?

3. If you <u>accuse</u> someone of stealing, are you saying he or she did something wrong?

4. Do people <u>contribute</u> cans and boxes of food to help feed others at Thanksgiving?

Write to the Point

Suppose that you went up in a hot air balloon over your neighborhood. Write a short paragraph describing the things you would see. Would you see a park? Would you see a pond or swimming pool? What would the place where you live look like from the air? Describe the size of the things you would see. Use spelling words from this lesson in your paragraph.

Challenge Use one or more of the Challenge Words in your paragraph.

Proofreading

Use the proofreading marks to show the errors in the paragraph below. Write the five misspelled words correctly in the blanks.

On a hike in maine, I spotted two truely beatiful deer. I wanted to take a picture of them, but i was to slow. Before I new it, they had run thrugh the bushes and were gone

◯	word is misspelled
⊙	period is missing
═	letter should be capitalized

1. _____

2. _____

3. _____

4. _____

5. _____

117

Lesson 22 Words with /ou/

Listen for /ou/ as you say each word.

ours

hours

sour

proud

cloud

counter

noun

south

mouth

loud

shower

crown

growl

crowd

crowded

tower

powerful

towel

vowel

somehow

1. Which words begin with the letter c?

_____ _____

_____

2. Which word begins with a vowel?

_____

3. Which word begins and ends with the same letter? _____

4. Write the words that end with the letter l.

_____ _____

_____ _____

5. Write the words that end with the letters th.

_____ _____

6. Which words end with the same four letters as flower? _____

_____

7. Which word ends with the same three letters as flour? _____

8. Which word begins and ends like load?

_____

9. Which word has the same beginning and ending sound as pride? _____

10. Which word begins with the letter h, but you don't hear /h/? _____

11. Write the compound word that ends with ow.

_____

Checkpoint

Write a spelling word for each clue.
Then use the Checkpoint Study Plan on page 224.

1. Chuckle is to giggle as grumble is to ___.

2. yours, mine, and ___

3. The opposite of north is ___.

4. floating along like a ___

5. Magician is to top hat as king is to ___.

6. When you do something well you feel ___.

7. not minutes, but ___

8. An absorbing cloth is a ___.

9. Full of people means ___.

10. Another word for strong is ___.

11. Two's company, three's a ___.

12. The opposite of sweet is ___.

13. as gentle as an April ___

14. Air is to nose as food is to ___.

15. Some way means ___.

16. A tall, narrow building is a ___.

17. When a noise isn't soft, it's ___.

18. Store items are displayed on a ___.

19-20. The first mystery word comes from the Latin word *nomen*, meaning name. It is a part of speech that names a person, place, thing, or idea. The second mystery word comes from the Latin word *vocalis*, meaning sound. It names letters that are not consonants. It also names the sounds made when we say these letters. Can you guess the mystery words?

___ ___

Wordsworth, the Word Wizard

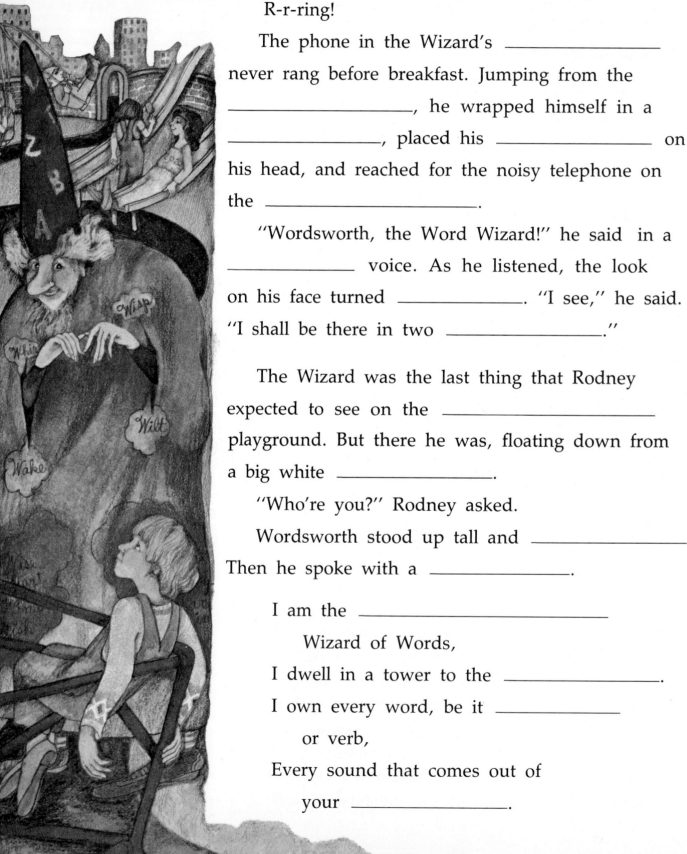

R-r-ring!

The phone in the Wizard's _____
never rang before breakfast. Jumping from the
_____, he wrapped himself in a
_____, placed his _____ on
his head, and reached for the noisy telephone on
the _____.

"Wordsworth, the Word Wizard!" he said in a
_____ voice. As he listened, the look
on his face turned _____. "I see," he said.
"I shall be there in two _____."

The Wizard was the last thing that Rodney
expected to see on the _____
playground. But there he was, floating down from
a big white _____.

"Who're you?" Rodney asked.

Wordsworth stood up tall and _____.
Then he spoke with a _____.

I am the _____
Wizard of Words,

I dwell in a tower to the _____.

I own every word, be it _____
or verb,

Every sound that comes out of
your _____.

120

"Well, what're ya doin' here? This playground is 'arz'!" Rodney huffed.

"_____! Not 'arz'! You! Not 'ya'!" said the Wizard.

"So I change a few sounds now and then. Big deal!" said Rodney.

"I'll show you what a big deal it is," said the Wizard. "I'll change a few sounds for you now and then." He snapped his fingers, cast a spell, and left in a puff of smoke.

"You just fry it. Go ahead and fry it!" Rodney stopped, puzzled. _____, every time he tried to say "try it," it came out "fry it." But that wasn't all! Sometimes, a consonant or _____ would change with no warning. Each time Rodney spoke, a _____ would gather and laugh.

But they felt sorry for him when he cried, "Where is that lizard?"

Well, being called a lizard was more than Wordsworth could stand. He came back.

"Have you had enough? Will you be more careful with words from now on?"

"I'll fry," Rodney sobbed.

"Good," said the Wizard and with a "snap," he removed the spell.

But as he drifted away, perhaps before the spell wore off, he heard Rodney's laughing voice call out, "Good-by, lizard!"

ours
hours
sour
proud
cloud
counter
noun
south
mouth
loud
shower
crown
growl
crowd
crowded
tower
powerful
towel
vowel
somehow

Quotation Marks

Put quotation marks around the exact words of a speaker. The first word in a direct quote begins with a capital letter.

"What letter of the alphabet do you drink?" asked Jill.
"I drink tea," Tom answered.

Tom asked, "What letter of the alphabet has a sting?"
Jill replied, "A bee stings."

★ Write the following sentences. Use quotation marks and capital letters where needed. Correct the misspelled words.

1. Faye said, I am so prowd of that team of ours.

_____

_____

2. they practice for three ours each day, said Brian.

_____

_____

3. a big croud always comes to the game, added Chris.

_____

_____

4. Leah said, sumhow they always seem to do their best.

_____

_____

5. even when they're behind, they never throw in the towle! Katie exclaimed. _____

_____

6. let's have a lowd cheer for them! shouted Ben. _____

_____

7. hip, hip, hooray! they shouted as their powerfull team ran onto the field. _____

_____

Challenge Yourself

drowsy counselor encounter blouse

Decide which Challenge Word fits each clue. Check your Spelling Dictionary to see if you were right. Then write sentences showing that you understand the meaning of each Challenge Word.

1. This is a person you go to for advice.

2. Seeing a friend in the hall at school and stopping to say hello is one of these.

3. A girl can tuck this piece of clothing into her jeans or a skirt.

4. It's how you feel early in the morning after staying up too late watching TV.

Write to the Point

When Wordsworth the Wizard didn't like something, he could simply snap his fingers to make it change. Is there something that you would change if you had Wordsworth's power? Write a paragraph telling what you would change, how you would change it, and why. Use spelling words from this lesson in your paragraph.

Challenge Use one or more of the Challenge Words in your paragraph.

Proofreading

Use the proofreading marks to show the errors in the paragraph below. Write the five misspelled words correctly in the blanks.

◯	word is misspelled
⚋	take out word
? / ∧	question mark is missing

We heard the wizard showt. Where was his towel He had put it on the cownter a few ours ago, but sumhow the it had disappeared. He called his servant with a groul.

1. _____

2. _____

3. _____

4. _____

5. _____

Lesson 23 Adding ed and ing

Say each spelling word.

asked

changed

pleased

caused

traded

invited

tasted

studied

copied

dried

cried

trying

carrying

swimming

beginning

jogging

closing

writing

hoping

saving

Solve these puzzles.

want + ed = <u>wanted</u>

1. ask + ed = _____

2. try + ing = _____

3. carry + ing = _____

vote − e + ed = <u>voted</u>

4. save − e + ing = _____

5. hope − e + ing = _____

6. close − e + ing = _____

7. write − e + ing = _____

8. trade − e + ed = _____

9. please − e + ed = _____

10. taste − e + ed = _____

11. change − e + ed = _____

12. cause − e + ed = _____

13. invite − e + ed = _____

carry − y + i + ed = <u>carried</u>

14. copy − y + i + ed = _____

15. dry − y + i + ed = _____

16. cry − y + i + ed = _____

17. study − y + i + ed = _____

skip + p + ing = <u>skipping</u>

18. swim + m + ing = _____

19. begin + n + ing = _____

20. jog + g + ing = _____

Checkpoint

Write a spelling word for each clue.
Then use the Checkpoint Study Plan on page 224.

1. Questioned means ___.

2. not the ending, but the ___

3. not unhappy, but ___

4. Sniffed is to smelled as ate is to ___.

5. Another word for running is ___.

6. The opposite of spending is ___.

7. Snow is to skiing as water is to ___.

8. If something becomes different, it has ___.

9. Ball game is to practiced as test is to ___.

10. To have made happen is to have ___.

11. Your attendance is requested means you're ___.

12. not dropping, but ___

13. Brush is to painting as pen is to ___.

14. Another word for swapped is ___.

15. The opposite of opening is ___.

16. Raisins are grapes that were ___.

17. wishing and ___

18. not laughed, but ___

19. Today I copy, yesterday I ___.

20. This mystery word usually means to make an effort. But this is only one of its meanings. The word comes from the Old French word *trier*. *Trier* means to select. This mystery word also means to select, to test, or to check out. Can you guess the word? Add the ending <u>ing</u> and you have the mystery word. ___

Patty and Her Pail

Use each word once to complete these pages.

One fine spring morning Patty went to market. She was _____ a pail of milk upon her head. As she walked along, she planned what she would do with the money she would get for the milk.

"First, I will buy some chicks from Farmer Jones," thought Patty. She was _____ that the chickens would lay many eggs. "Then I will sell the eggs at the market."

Patty thought and thought. She was _____ to figure out exactly how much money she would make, and how she'd spend it.

"With the money I get from the sale of the eggs," she went on, "I shall buy a pretty new dress and a beautiful new hat. When I go to market, everyone will look at me!"

_____ her eyes, Patty saw herself as the prettiest girl in town. Feeling very _____ with herself, she said, "When they see my new clothes, I'll just look at them and toss my head back like this . . ."

And just as she was _____ to toss her head back, the pail fell off it. All the milk spilled on the ground.

"Look what my dreaming has _____ to happen," she _____.

Don't count your chickens before they hatch!

126

The Tortoise and the Hare

A hare once boasted that he was the fastest of all animals and _____ anyone to challenge him.

"Why not race against me?" _____ the tortoise.

So the hare went _____ down the road, sure of winning. Soon the hare slowed down and _____ the pace of the tortoise, making fun of him. But the tortoise never _____ his steady pace.

When the hare saw a pond, he decided to go _____. Then the tortoise _____ places with the hare, taking the lead. The hare came out of the water and _____ himself off in the sun. He _____ some berries and relaxed in the shade. He was _____ his energy for the end of the race. But when he ran to the finish line, the tortoise had already crossed it!

And people have _____ this story and have been _____ about it ever since!

asked
changed
pleased
caused
traded
invited
tasted
studied
copied
dried
cried
trying
carrying
swimming
beginning
jogging
closing
writing
hoping
saving

FINISH

Predicates

The predicate is the part of a sentence that tells what the subject has done or is doing. Predicates usually begin with a verb.

The little girl skipped down the street.

Skipped down the street is the predicate of this sentence.

 ★Find the predicate in each sentence. Then write it.

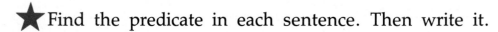

1. Last summer I invited my cousin to our house.

   _____

2. We swam in the pool. _____

3. Then we changed into shorts and T-shirts. _____

4. We jogged in the park until lunch time. _____

   _____

5. Lunch tasted great! _____

6. We traded our favorite mystery stories. _____

   _____

7. We both cried when vacation was over! _____

   _____

Often a predicate has an action verb and a helping verb.

My friends are jogging to keep fit.

Jogging is the action verb. Are is the helping verb.
Are jogging to keep fit is the predicate.

★Write the predicate for each sentence.

8. She is writing a letter. _____

9. I am saving it. _____

WORDS AT WORK

Challenge Yourself

hustled	importing
overlapping	fortified

What do you think each underlined Challenge Word means? Check your Spelling Dictionary to see if you are right. Then write sentences showing that you understand the meaning of each Challenge Word.

1. Because I overslept, I <u>hustled</u> to meet the school bus on time.

2. The United States is <u>importing</u> oil from several countries.

3. Be sure the edges of the tent are <u>overlapping</u> so rain can't get in.

4. During the flood, we <u>fortified</u> the banks of the river with sandbags.

Write to the Point

Did you ever make a mistake that taught you a useful lesson? Write a story to tell what happened and what you learned. At the end of your story, write a sentence that tells what you learned, such as "Be prepared for emergencies!" or "Showing off is never smart." Use spelling words from this lesson in your story.

Challenge Use one or more of the Challenge Words in your story.

Proofreading

Use the proofreading marks to show the errors in the paragraph below. Write the five misspelled words correctly in the blanks.

Here's the begining of a story. Mrs Duck was swiming in the pond. mr. Fox invited her to dinner. She was pleazed. She aksed what he would serve. try riting his answer.

⬭	word is misspelled
⊙	period is missing
☰	letter should be capitalized

1. _____

2. _____

3. _____

4. _____

5. _____

Lesson 24 Words in Review

A. wonderful
discover
stomach
once
blood

B. sugar
pudding
woman
should
understood

C. choose
knew
truly
route
fruit
through
two
beautiful

D. loud
crowd

★ **Use a piece of paper for the starred activities.**

1. In Lesson 19 you studied two ways to spell /ŭ/: o, oo. Write the words in list A.

_____   _____

_____   _____

2. In Lesson 20 you studied four ways to spell /ŏŏ/: oo, u, ou, o. Write the words in list B.

_____   _____

_____   _____

_____

★**3.** Now write a sentence for each review word in lists A and B.

4. In Lesson 21 you studied six ways to spell /ōō/: oo, ou, ew, u, ui, o; and one way to spell /yōō/: eau. Write the words in list C.

_____   _____

_____   _____

_____   _____

5. In Lesson 22 you studied two ways to spell /ou/: ou, ow. Write the words in list D.

_____   _____

★**6.** Write the words in lists C and D. Look up each word in the Spelling Dictionary and write the sound spelling beside each word.

★**7.** Write all 20 review words in alphabetical order.

★**8.** Divide the words you wrote into syllables.

Writer's Workshop

A Description

A description tells about a person, place, or thing. It includes details that can help a reader know exactly what you are describing. Try to appeal to your reader's senses—sight, sound, smell, touch, and taste—when you write a description. Here is Carlotta's description of a birthday cake.

A Cake to Remember

The cake was covered with fluffy white frosting and topped with roses made of pink, yellow, and green frosting. A white candle stood in each rose. Beneath the frosting were two layers of dark cake with a sticky brown filling between them. The filling smelled like chocolate and had crunchy nuts and chewy bits of coconut in it.

To write her description, Carlotta followed the steps in the writing process. She began with a **Prewriting** activity using a senses web. There she wrote down all of the things about the cake that she could see, smell, touch, and taste. Part of Carlotta's senses web is shown here. Study what Carlotta did.

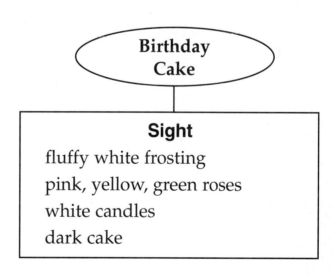

Birthday Cake

Sight
fluffy white frosting
pink, yellow, green roses
white candles
dark cake

Get ready to write your own description. You can describe a kind of food, an object in your home, a place, or anything else. After you have decided what to write about, make a senses web and fill it in with details about your topic. Then follow the other steps in the writing process—**Writing, Revising, Proofreading,** and **Publishing.**

Lesson 25 Words with /oi/

Listen for /oi/ as you say each word.

spoil
coin
point
choice
noise
voice
avoid
join
soil
poison
moisture

enjoy
destroy
employ
employer
loyal
royal
voyage
loyalty
soybean

1. Write the one-syllable words that end with the letter <u>l</u>. _____

_____

2. Write the two-syllable words that end with the letter <u>l</u>. _____

_____

3. Which words end with /s/? _____

_____

4. Which word ends with /z/? _____

5. Write the two-syllable words that begin with a vowel. _____

_____   _____

6. Write the two-syllable words in which you hear /oi/ in the first syllable. _____

_____

_____

7. Which word begins with the letter <u>j</u>?

_____

8. Write the word in which you see the letter <u>c</u> but hear /k/. _____

9. Which word begins like <u>pet</u> and ends like <u>joint</u>?

_____

10. Which word begins and ends like <u>decoy</u>?

_____

11. Write the words that have three syllables.

_____

Checkpoint

Write a spelling word for each clue.
Then use the Checkpoint Study Plan on page 224.

1. Another word for earth is ___.

2. The opposite of quit is ___.

3. A penny is a ___.

4. trip or journey ___

5. Fruit is to apple as vegetable is to ___.

6. To hire is to ___.

7. Brave is to bravery as loyal is to ___.

8. Insecticide is an insect ___.

9. ruin, or ___

10. the singer's high-pitched ___

11. to ruin completely, leaving nothing left ___

12. The opposite of quiet is ___.

13. A boss is an ___.

14. Faithful means ___.

15. To get away from means to ___.

16. To like is to ___.

17. Dew is water, or ___.

18. selection, or ___

19. The pencil has a sharp ___.

20. There are three English words that mean fit for a king. One is from Old English. One is from Latin. One is from French. Each comes from the word for king in its own language. <u>Kingly</u> is from the Old English word king. <u>Regal</u> is from the Latin word *rex*. The mystery word is from the French *roi*. Can you guess the mystery word? ___

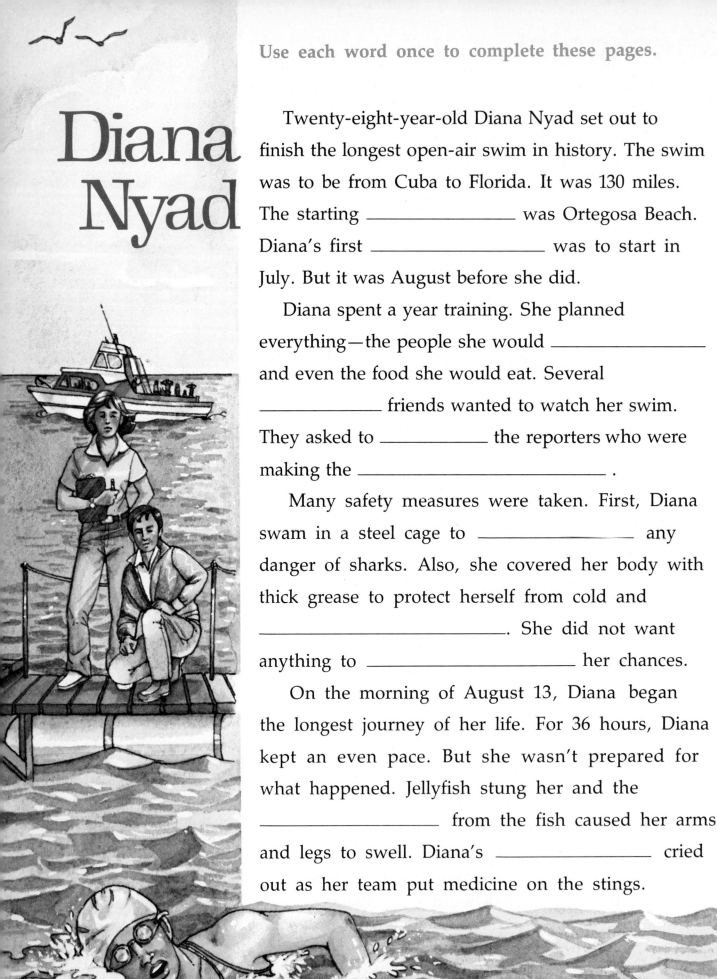

Diana Nyad

Use each word once to complete these pages.

Twenty-eight-year-old Diana Nyad set out to finish the longest open-air swim in history. The swim was to be from Cuba to Florida. It was 130 miles. The starting _____ was Ortegosa Beach. Diana's first _____ was to start in July. But it was August before she did.

Diana spent a year training. She planned everything—the people she would _____ and even the food she would eat. Several _____ friends wanted to watch her swim. They asked to _____ the reporters who were making the _____ .

Many safety measures were taken. First, Diana swam in a steel cage to _____ any danger of sharks. Also, she covered her body with thick grease to protect herself from cold and _____ . She did not want anything to _____ her chances.

On the morning of August 13, Diana began the longest journey of her life. For 36 hours, Diana kept an even pace. But she wasn't prepared for what happened. Jellyfish stung her and the _____ from the fish caused her arms and legs to swell. Diana's _____ cried out as her team put medicine on the stings.

As the hours passed, it became hard for Diana to hold down food. Six-foot waves knocked against her cage. The wind and waves became so rough that the boat was thrown off course. After 41 hours, she was pulled from the water. But nothing could _____ this dream.

One year later, she became the first person to swim the 60 miles between Florida and the Bahamas. As she set foot on the _____ of Juno Beach, Diana was given a _____ welcome. She was greeted by the _____ of boat whistles and the cheers of fans.

After stopping to _____ her victory, Diana said that she'd try the "Cuba to Florida" course again. If she made it, it would be her last long-distance swim.

- Reporters were impressed with the great
_____ of Diana's crew.

- Diana was more than just an
_____ to them.

- Many athletes eat food made from
_____ flour.

- Long ago, a metal _____ might have a picture of an athlete on it.

135

spoil
coin
point
choice
noise
voice
avoid
join
soil
poison
moisture
enjoy
destroy
employ
employer
loyal
royal
voyage
loyalty
soybean

Entry Words

Entry words in a dictionary are often more than one part of speech. Sometimes, the parts of speech are all listed within one entry. At other times, they are listed in separate entries.

---

soil¹ | soil | *n.* **1.** The loose top layer of the earth's surface, suitable for the growth of plant life. **2.** A particular kind of earth or ground: *sandy soil.* **3.** Country; region: *native soil.* —**modifier:** *soil erosion.*

soil² | soil | *v.* **1.** To make or become dirty. **2.** To disgrace; tarnish: *soil one's reputation.*

---

voy·age | voi′ĭj | *n.* A long journey to a distant place, made on a ship, boat, etc., or sometimes an aircraft or spacecraft: *Columbus' four voyages to the New World; a voyage up the Hudson; a voyage to the moon.* —*v.* **voy·aged, voy·ag·ing.** To travel by making a voyage. —**voy′ag·er** *n.*

---

1. Which word has only one entry? _____

2. Which word has two separate entries? _____

Soil has two separate entries because the noun comes from the Latin word meaning <u>ground</u> and the verb comes from the Latin word meaning <u>pig</u>. When the origin of the word is different for each part of speech, different entries are given.

★ These words can be either nouns or verbs. Use them to complete the sentences. Then write noun or verb after each.

point   noise   poison   spoil   voice

3. If milk is not kept cold, it will _____ .

   noun or verb _____

4. After recess, the _____ in the playground stopped.

   noun or verb _____

5. Can you _____ that flashlight along the path?

   noun or verb _____

6. Bottles containing _____ are clearly marked.

   noun or verb _____

7. Her _____ could be heard above all the others.

   noun or verb _____

WORDS AT WORK

Challenge Yourself

appoint   poise   pointless   toil

Decide which Challenge Word fits each clue. Check your Spelling Dictionary to see if you were right. Then write sentences showing that you understand the meaning of each Challenge Word.

1. People who have this are calm under pressure. People without it may get very excited.

2. To pull weeds all day in the hot sun is to do this.

3. This word tells what it is like to try to teach a fish to talk.

4. This is one way a teacher can get a helper.

Write to the Point

Diana Nyad thought about safety as she planned her long-distance swim. What safety rules do you follow when you take part in sports or hobbies? Write a list of safety rules for a sport, such as biking. Or write a list of rules for a hobby, such as cooking. Use words from this spelling lesson in your rules.

Challenge Use one or more of the Challenge Words in your rules.

Proofreading

Use the proofreading marks to show the errors in the paragraph below. Write the five misspelled words correctly in the blanks.

The noize of the crowd rises as joe crosses finish line. At this point his loyel fans run to joine him. They want to help him injoy his win. They know he wouldn't spoyl perfect record.

◯	word is misspelled
≡	letter should be capitalized
∧	word is missing

1. _____

2. _____

3. _____

4. _____

5. _____

Lesson 26 Words with /ô/

Listen for /ô/ as you say each word.

pause
cause
because
author
applaud
autumn
daughter
caught
taught

strong
wrong
coffee
office
often
offer
gone

thought
bought
brought

already

1. Write the two-syllable words that begin with a vowel. _____

_____

_____

2. Write the words that end with /z/.

_____

_____

3. Write the words that end with the letters er.

_____

4. Write the words that end with /ē/.

_____

5. Which words end with the letters ought?

_____

_____

6. Which word begins with the letter g?

_____

7. Which word begins with three consonants?

_____

8. Write the word in which you see the letter n but don't hear /n/. _____

9. Write the word in which you see the letter w but don't hear /w/. _____

10. Which words end with the letters aught?

_____

11. Which word ends with /ər/ but not the letters er? _____

Checkpoint

Write a spelling word for each clue.
Then use the Checkpoint Study Plan on page 224.

1. Today I teach, yesterday I ___.

2. The opposite of weak is ___.

3. Another word for the fall season is ___.

4. Someone who writes a book is an ___.

5. What made something happen is its ___.

6. The opposite of seldom is ___.

7. Today I buy, yesterday I ___.

8. To present means to ___.

9. A rat in a trap has been ___.

10. For the reason that, means why or ___.

11. A place where people work at desks is an ___.

12. Father is to son as mother is to ___.

13. Paid-for advice is a bought ___.

14. If I clap, then I ___.

15. Today I bring, yesterday I ___.

16. After John leaves, John is ___.

17. not right, but ___

18. To stop briefly is to ___.

19. If it is done by now, it is done ___.

20. The origin of this word is not certain. It names a bean and the drink made from this bean. Some believe it comes from the Arabic word *qaveh*, meaning a strong drink. Today the beans are ground up. Hot water is forced through the grounds to make a hot, strong drink. Can you guess the word that names the drink? ___

Lorraine Hansberry

Lorraine Hansberry was born in Chicago, Illinois, on May 19, 1930. She was the youngest _____ of Carl and Nannie Hansberry. By the time she was 13, Lorraine _____ knew she wanted a job in the theater. After high school, she went to college. There she learned about great writers and was _____ how to put on plays. Soon, she began writing her own plays and moved to New York City.

At first, Lorraine wasn't able to earn money as an _____. She took odd jobs. First, she was a clerk in an _____. Then she waited on tables in a _____ shop, where people _____ breakfast and lunch. In the _____ of 1957,

Lorraine read her friends part of a play she'd just written. When she finished, her friends began to
_____. They _____
the play to some theater people who agreed to put it on. It was called A Raisin in the Sun.

Lorraine had _____ feelings about equal rights. She _____ that it was _____ to judge people because of their race. The actors in her play talked about those ideas. People were moved _____ of the way the feelings of black Americans were explained on the stage. They were also moved because Lorraine was only 28 years old! The play became a great hit. Lorraine Hansberry became the youngest woman and the first black woman to receive a prize for "Best Play." Soon, a film company made her an _____ to make a movie of her play.

Lorraine then became _____ up in the civil rights movement. Because it was a _____ she believed in, she started writing a book about it. But she became ill and had to _____ in her work.

In January, 1965, Lorraine Hansberry died. Even though she is _____, her work still remains. The movie A Raisin in the Sun is _____ shown on TV. A few years ago, friends of Lorraine Hansberry produced a play, To Be Young, Gifted, and Black, about her life.

141

Capitals

The first word, last word, and other important words in a title are capitalized. Small words, such as <u>a</u>, <u>the</u>, <u>in</u>, <u>to</u>, and <u>of</u>, are not capitalized when they are in the middle of a title. This is true of titles of books, stories, songs, movies, and television programs.

"The Fox and the Grapes"

<u>*The Prince and the Pauper*</u>

★ Write the sentences below. Correct any spelling errors in the sentences and the capitalization errors in the titles.

1. My favorite book is <u>gonne with the Wind</u>. _____

2. E. B. White is the awthor of <u>the trumpet of The Swan</u>. _____

_____

3. The library has a beautiful book of photographs called <u>the colors of autum</u>. _____

_____

4. I took this book out of the library because <u>All about cats</u> was olready taken. _____

_____

5. Our music teacher taught us the words to "city Of New Orleans" for our next assembly. _____

_____

6. I can't sing my solo in "Sing, sing a song" because I cawght a cold. _____

Challenge Yourself

auction	audio
precaution	offerings

Use your Spelling Dictionary to answer these questions. Then write sentences showing that you understand the meaning of each Challenge Word.

1. Does audio equipment help people see?

2. Can people buy things at an auction?

3. If you give cans of food to help homeless people, are the cans of food your offerings?

4. Is locking the door a precaution against getting sick?

Write to the Point

Lorraine Hansberry won a prize for writing a very good play. What kind of an award or prize would you like to win? Would it be an award for something you wrote? In a short paragraph, tell about the award or prize that you would like to win. Use spelling words from this lesson in your paragraph.

Challenge Use one or more of the Challenge Words in your paragraph.

Proofreading

Use the proofreading marks to show the errors in the paragraph below. Write the five misspelled words correctly in the blanks.

mrs. Chong went to the box ofice on main Street and baught tickets for the play Sleeping Beauty She thought her daugter would enjoy the play becawse she offen reads fairy tales.

⬭	word is misspelled
⊙	period is missing
≡	letter should be capitalized

1. _____

2. _____

3. _____

4. _____

5. _____

Lesson 27 Words with /ô/

Listen for /ô/ as you say each word.

morning
north
popcorn
report
orbit
important
chorus
shore
before
explore
score

straw
lawn
yawn
crawl
dawn

toward
warm
quart
water

1. Which words begin with the letter w?

_____

2. Write the one-syllable words that end with the letter n.

_____

_____

3. Which word begins with /kw/?

_____

4. Write the word in which you see the letters ch but hear /k/. _____

5. Which words end with the same three letters as chore?

_____

_____

6. Which word ends with the same four letters as forth? _____

7. Which word ends with the same three letters as sprawl? _____

8. Which word ends with ing?

_____

9. Which word begins with three consonants?

_____

10. Write the word that begins with the letter t.

_____

11. Write the words that end with the letter t.

_____

_____

12. Write the compound word that begins with the letter p. _____

144

Checkpoint

Write a spelling word for each clue.
Then use the Checkpoint Study Plan on page 224.

1. If you're tired or bored, you might ___.
2. A company of singers is a ___.
3. The winning team has the higher ___.
4. not cool, but ___
5. If it matters a lot, then it is ___.
6. As the sun comes up, the day begins to ___.
7. After the sun comes up, it is ___.
8. The oceans are filled with ___.
9. The moon moves around the earth in an ___.
10. The news from the harbor is a seaport ___.
11. If you cut the grass, then you mow the ___.
12. Before you can walk, you must ___.
13. The opposite of south is ___.
14. Cup is to pint as pint is to ___.
15. not after, but ___
16. not away from, but ___
17. Water is to pipe as milk is to ___.
18. At the movie I ate ___.
19. To search for is to ___.

20. This mystery word names a strip of land along
the edge of a body of water. It comes from the
Old English word *sceran*. *Sceran* meant to cut.
What's the connection? The mystery word
originally meant the strip that cuts off the water
from the land. See the connection? Now guess
the mystery word. ___

145

Mysteries for the Moonship

One _____, Mr. Goodkind had a scavenger hunt for his class. Teams were named and given a list of things to find. The team named the Moonship (Kit, Nahal, Nick, and Ellen) began to groan. The Moonship's list was hidden in three riddles. Nick read the first riddle:

Let the pan go from _____ to hot,
While into _____ I am shot.
Sputter, sputter, pour on the butter!

"Let's go!" Kit said. "Maybe the answer will pop into our heads. Pop . . . _____!"

"Popcorn's the answer!" they shouted.

So the Moonship headed _____ Nahal's house to get some popcorn. They found a _____ of milk and drank it. They washed the milk carton with _____ and put the popcorn in. The second riddle was harder:

From _____ to dark I nibble
and _____.
I've a soft fuzzy body that's low and small.
When the time comes I spin a soft wrap.
I _____ and curl up inside for a nap.
I wake up and am not what I was before.
On beautiful wings, I've the sky
to _____.

146

"A baby takes a nap and crawls," said Nahal.

"Hey, Kit! Stop eating our popcorn. This is

_____. Think!"

"I am thinking about how good this popcorn would taste if it were buttered . . . buttered? Butterfly!"

"No. But caterpillar is the answer!" said Nick.

The Moonship team found a caterpillar near the

_____ of Emmet Lake. From there, they headed _____ to Ellen's house.

Ellen read the next riddle:

In spring, I rise, damp and green,
In _____ and field I am seen.
Yet soon,
I'm a basket, I'm a hat.
I'm a broom, I'm a welcome mat.
Scarecrows and haystacks are made from me.
Burning matches I hate to see.

"_____!" the Moonship sang out in

_____, as they grabbed a broom from

the kitchen.

With a straw broom, the caterpillar, and the popcorn they raced back to school. Soon, they arrived in their classroom to _____

their good _____.

"Kids," Mr. Goodkind said. "You got here

_____ the others. It looks like the

Moonship made the first landing!"

147

morning
north
popcorn
report
orbit
important
chorus
shore
before
explore
score
straw
lawn
yawn
crawl
dawn
toward
warm
quart
water

Commas

Use commas in a friendly letter:

in the date, between the day of the month and the year

February 29, 1984

after the last word of the greeting

Dear Ebeneezer,

after the last word of the closing

Your friend,

★ Add commas to the date, greeting, and closing in the two letters below. Also, find the misspelled words in each letter and write them correctly.

June 23 199___

Dear Deb

    We're here at the lake and it's really great. Our cabin is right on the sure. Tomorrow morening, I plan to eksplore the woods around us.

                           Yours truly
                           Dawn

June 25 199___

Dear Dawn

    It has been really worm here. Today I went to the pool. The watter felt great.

    While I was mowing the lown yesterday, your dog ate my mom's favorite flowers. I guess that's all I have to repourt.

                           Yours truly
                           Deb

Challenge Yourself

adorn   awesome   hoard   torture

What do you think each underlined Challenge Word means? Check your Spelling Dictionary to see if you are right. Then write sentences showing that you understand the meaning of each Challenge Word.

1. Clara eats all the jellybeans she finds, but William likes to <u>hoard</u> his in a secret place.

2. The view from the mountain was an <u>awesome</u> sight.

3. We decided to <u>adorn</u> the class float with ribbons and flowers.

4. It was <u>torture</u> to hike five miles in the hot sun.

Write to the Point

Mr. Goodkind made his students think by giving them riddles that described different things. Write two riddles like Mr. Goodkind wrote for the scavenger hunt. Then see if your classmates can guess what you have described in your riddles. Use spelling words from this lesson in your riddles.

Challenge Use one or more of the Challenge Words in your riddles.

Proofreading

Use the proofreading marks to show the errors in the paragraph below. Write the five misspelled words correctly in the blanks.

⬭	word is misspelled
⊙	period is missing
⤙	take out word

One mornning Mr Goodkind took his students to the shor. They piled off the bus with a a choras of cheers. Then they ran tord the water to explore They had never been to the beach befour.

1. _____

2. _____

3. _____

4. _____

5. _____

Lesson 28 Words with /ä/ and /â/

Listen for /ä/ and /â/ as you say each word.

sharp

marbles

smart

large

scarf

apart

alarm

heart

careful

square

fare

stares

share

air

fair

stairs

there

where

their

they're

1. Which words begin with a vowel?

_____

_____

2. Which words begin with the letters th? Circle the word that contains an apostrophe.

_____

_____

3. Which word begins with the letter h?

_____

4. Which words end with /z/?

_____

_____

5. Which words end with the letters are?

_____

_____

6. Which word begins like fat and ends with the letters air? _____

7. Write the word in which you hear /hw/.

_____

8. Which word begins like smile and ends with the same three letters as part? _____

9. Which word ends with the same three letters as harp? _____

10. Write the word that ends with /j/.

_____

11. Solve these: sc + arf = _____

care + ful = _____

Checkpoint

Write a spelling word for each clue.
Then use the Checkpoint Study Plan on page 224.

1. The opposite of small is ____.

2. a game using small round objects ____

3. not round, but ____

4. The short way to say they are is ____.

5. A portion of something is a ____.

6. If I pay for a bus ride, then I pay a ____.

7. A broad band of cloth you wear is a ____.

8. If you treat people well, then you are ____.

9. If you have arrived, then you are ____.

10. A smoke detector in the barn is a farm ____.

11. Directions tell you how; maps tell you ____.

12. as free as the ____

13. You walk up a flight of ____.

14. not together, but ____

15. not dull, but ____

16. Another word for intelligent is ____.

17. The opposite of careless is ____.

18. She is to her as they is to ____.

19. If he gazes, then he ____.

20. An idiom is a group of words with a special meaning. You may know what each word in the idiom means. But that won't tell you what the idiom itself means. This mystery word is used in several idioms. The idiom to break someone's _?_ means to cause someone a lot of grief. To know something by _?_ means to have it memorized. Guess the mystery word. ____

The Marble Contest

Charles woke at once to the sound of the

_____. It was the morning of the marble

contest. Charles reached under his bed for his prize

_____. He wrapped a handful in

his mother's old red _____, dressed

quickly, and ran down the _____ to

grab some breakfast.

"Got everything you need?" his mother asked.

"You bet, Ma. I've got my best marbles ready to

go. My lucky one is packed in a box. Can't take a

chance losing that one!"

"Oh, Charles! You're a _____ boy.

You should know that it isn't luck that wins a

game," his mother said.

Charles ate his breakfast and gathered his

belongings. He was _____ as he

lifted the small _____ box that held

his lucky marble.

The crisp autumn _____ hummed with

excitement and Charles' _____ pounded

as he got closer to the center of town. A very

_____ group of boys had gathered in

the village square. _____ faces glowed

as Charles came near. He met their _____.

After all, he was the champion!

"Look at that crowd over _____,"
his friend Jess shouted. "_____
waiting for us."

The boys gathered around the circle. Charles
tapped his pocket and felt the small square box.
Soon, the boys were shooting marbles with quick,
_____ flicks of their fingers. When the
marbles were knocked _____, laughs
and shouts would go through the group.

As the day wore on, players were eliminated.
Charles and Jess were alone around the circle. Those
who lost stayed to _____ the thrill of
the last match. Charles pulled out the box to place
his lucky marble beside him.

"This isn't my lucky marble," he shouted.
"_____ is my tiger's-eye marble? Hold
on! This isn't _____."

But Jess wanted the game to go on.

"How could I have done this?" Charles
wondered. "O.K., Ma. Now let's see what skill
can do!"

He aimed his marble at the center and closed his
eyes. The marbles clicked and a cheer came from
the crowd.

"The winner and still champion, Charles
Coleman!"

Charles' prize was his _____ to the
statewide marble contest in St. Louis.

sharp
marbles
smart
large
scarf
apart
alarm
heart
careful
square
fare
stares
share
air
fair
stairs
there
where
their
they're

Pronunciation

A dictionary lists a pronunciation for each entry word. This pronunciation or sound spelling is written in special symbols.

> **pro·nun·ci·a·tion** | prə nŭn′sē ā′shən | *n.* **1.** The act or manner of pronouncing words. **2.** A phonetic representation of a word, showing how it is pronounced. —*modifier: a pronunciation key.*

★ Look up the following words in the Spelling Dictionary. Write each word and its sound spelling.

1. scarf _____

2. sharp _____

3. stairs _____

To understand the sound symbols better, look at the pronunciation key on page 196. The key gives examples of words that have the sound of the symbols.

★ Write the key words for these symbols.

4. â _____   **5.** ä _____

6. ă _____   **7.** ā _____

★ The words below are followed by two sound spellings, one correct and one incorrect. Look up each word in the Spelling Dictionary. Write each word and its correct sound spelling.

8. square /skwâr/ /skär/ _____

9. where /wāre/ /hwâr/ _____

10. careful /**kâr**′fəl/ /**cār**′fəl/ _____

11. heart /hêrt/ /härt/ _____

12. alarm /ə **lärm**′/ /ə **lâm**′/ _____

13. air /âr/ /ār/ _____

Challenge Yourself

collage	airborne
regardless	varnish

What do you think each underlined Challenge Word means? Check your Spelling Dictionary to see if you are right. Then write sentences showing that you understand the meaning of each Challenge Word.

1. We used string, colored paper, and buttons to make a collage to hang on the wall.

2. I could not see the airborne dust, but it made me sneeze.

3. The picnic will be held today regardless of the weather.

4. The coat of varnish made the desk shine as if it were new.

Write to the Point

Sometimes the simplest games, like marbles, jacks, and tag, are the most fun to play. Think of a game you know that is simple enough to explain in a few sentences. Then write instructions telling how to play it. Make your instructions easy for a beginner to follow. Use spelling words from this lesson in your instructions.

Challenge Use one or more of the Challenge Words in your instructions.

Proofreading

Use the proofreading marks to show the errors in the paragraph below. Write the five misspelled words correctly in the blanks.

I count to fifty and take the skarf away. Where is pat Am I smeart enough to find him? He's not under the stares. I push some larje bushes apart, and their he is.

◯	word is misspelled
≡	letter should be capitalized
?∧	question mark is missing

1. _____

2. _____

3. _____

4. _____

5. _____

Lesson 29 Plurals, Possessives

Say each word.

men

women

children

feet

teeth

sheep

oxen

mice

geese

wives

knives

shelves

man's

men's

woman's

women's

child's

children's

wife's

cloud's

Some nouns form plurals in an irregular way.
Write the plural form of:

1. wife _____

2. shelf _____

3. knife _____

4. man _____

5. ox _____

6. foot _____

7. woman _____

8. mouse _____

9. tooth _____

10. child _____

11. goose _____

12. sheep _____

Singular nouns form possessives by adding 's.
Write the possessive form of:

13. man _____

14. woman _____

15. child _____

16. wife _____

17. cloud _____

Plural nouns that do not end in s form the
possessive by adding 's. Write the possessive of:

18. men _____

19. women _____

20. children _____

Checkpoint

Write a spelling word for each clue.
Then use the Checkpoint Study Plan on page 224.

1. It belongs to the men. It is the ___.

2. If it belongs to the man, it is the ___.

3. If it belongs to the woman, it is the ___.

4. If it comes from the cloud, it is the ___.

5. Another word for boys and girls is ___.

6. I set the table with forks, spoons, and ___.

7. If children have bikes, the bikes are the ___.

8. It's not the husband's, but the ___.

9. If it belongs to the child, it is the ___.

10. Dishes are to cabinets as books are to ___.

11. If it belongs to all the women, it is the ___.

12. not men, but ___

13. They were as quiet as ___.

14. Animals that provide wool are ___.

15. When I smile I show my ___.

16. Boys grow up to be ___.

17. one ox, two ___

18. not hands, but ___

19. chicks, ducks, ___

20. Long ago this word simply meant a woman. It comes from the Old English word *wif*. *Wif* was often used to describe a woman who sold something. A woman who sold fish was a *fischwif*. A woman who sold apples was an *applewif*. Today, the word means a married woman. Guess the word. Its plural is the mystery word. ___

157

In Someone Else's Shoes

There once lived a man named Sten who had a wife, Inga, and four _____. Every day, Sten worked in the fields, like the other _____. And like the other _____, Inga stayed at home.

One day, Sten said that his work was hard, while his _____ work was easy. Inga said, "I wonder what would happen if husbands and _____ traded places."

Sten laughed. "Let's trade work and you will see how hard a _____ life really is."

His wife answered, "And you may discover that a _____ life is not so easy, either."

So Inga hitched up the _____ and set off for the fields.

In the meantime, Sten began to make the _____ breakfast and told them to brush their _____. As soon as Sten had taken care of one _____ needs, it seemed that another wanted his help. So he left the house and began his chores.

First, he fed the cows. Then he scattered grain for the _____. Sten didn't feed the cats since they were busy chasing the _____. Just as he began to put the _____ out to pasture, he heard the children yelling. Sten didn't know how he could watch both the children and the sheep.

So he carried the sheep up to the roof to graze. He tied ropes around their legs and dropped the ropes down the chimney. He rushed to the kitchen and tied a rope around each of his legs so that the sheep could not run away. Sten washed the dishes, the _____, and the forks. He began to put them on the kitchen _____ when he felt the ropes pulling him. The sheep had fallen and Sten went _____ first up the chimney. His eyes looked out over the cold logs.

In the fields, Inga stopped working. The sun was covered by a _____ shape. All the men were heading home. Judging that her wagon was as full as the _____ wagons, she went home, too.

When she opened the door, Inga saw Sten hanging upside down in the fireplace and the children running wildly about. Quickly, she grabbed a knife and cut the rope.

"Well," she asked, "how would you like to do _____ work every day?"

And Sten never said a word about "women's work" again.

159

men
women
children
feet
teeth
sheep
oxen
mice
geese
wives
knives
shelves
man's
men's
woman's
women's
child's
children's
wife's
cloud's

Apostrophes

An apostrophe is used to show the possessive form of a word. Add 's to a singular noun to make it possessive.

the boy's hat = the hat that belongs to the boy
the child's toy = the toy that belongs to the child

To form the possessive of a plural noun that already ends with the letter s, add only an apostrophe.

The boys' sleds are red.

If a plural noun does not end in s, add 's to form the possessive.

The children's sleds are fast.

Choose the correct word for each sentence.

woman's   women   women's

1. This _____ car has broken down.
2. Those two _____ jog every morning.
3. These _____ gardens are beautiful.

child's   children   children's

4. The _____ all play together.
5. Three _____ lunches were missing.
6. One _____ jacket is ripped.

This sign is for a garage sale. Correct the possessives.

2 rocking chairs
1 large mirror
1 mans' hat
5 pairs of mens' shoes
1 womans' winter coat
1 childs' roller skates

7. _____

8. _____

9. _____

10. _____

Challenge Yourself

larvae thieves mongoose's patios

Decide which Challenge Word fits each clue. Check your Spelling Dictionary to see if you were right. Then write sentences showing that you understand the meaning of each Challenge Word.

1. They take things that don't belong to them.

2. These are places outside where you can relax.

3. This means belonging to a kind of furry animal that kills snakes.

4. These will soon change into something very different.

Write to the Point

Think about the things you can do very well. Then think about a job you might want to have someday. It can be a job done by someone you know. Or it can be one you make up. Write a paragraph telling about the job and why you chose it. Use spelling words from the lesson in your paragraph.

Challenge Use one or more of the Challenge Words in your paragraph.

Proofreading

Use the proofreading marks to show the errors in the paragraph below. Write the five misspelled words correctly in the blanks.

◯	word is misspelled
≡	letter should be capitalized
∧	word is missing

In the beginning sten thought a mans work was hard. Cleaning shelfs and feeding geese must easy. Anyone can put knivs on a shelf or watch the sheeps. In the end he wanted drive the oxan again.

1. _____

2. _____

3. _____

4. _____

5. _____

Lesson 30 Words in Review

A. choice
loyal

B. autumn
daughter
wrong
gone
already
bought

C. important
explore
toward
dawn
water

D. scarf
heart

E. square
fair
where
their
they're

★Use a piece of paper for the starred activities.

1. In Lesson 25 you studied two ways to spell /oi/: oi, oy. Write the words in list A.

_____   _____

2. In Lesson 26 you studied four ways to spell /ô/: au, o, ou, a. Write the words in list B.

_____   _____

_____   _____

★**3.** Now write a sentence for each review word in lists A and B.

4. In Lesson 27 you studied three ways to spell /ô/: o, aw, a. Write the words in list C.

_____   _____

_____   _____

5. In Lesson 28 you studied two ways to spell /ä/: a, ea. Write the words in list D.

_____   _____

6. You also studied five different ways to spell /â/: a, ai, e, ei, ey. Write the words in list E.

_____   _____

_____   _____

★**7.** Look up each word in lists C, D, and E, and write the first definition beside it.

★**8.** Write all 20 review words in alphabetical order.

★**9.** Divide the words you wrote into syllables.

Writer's Workshop

Instructions

Instructions tell a reader how to do something. A good set of instructions carefully describes each step that must be followed. The writer must not confuse the reader by leaving out something important. Words like <u>first</u>, <u>then</u>, and <u>next</u>, can help the reader move from step to step. Here are Arturo's instructions on how to stand on your head.

How to Stand on Your Head

Standing on your head is easy once you get the feel of it. First, get on your knees and put the top of your forehead on a pillow. Then put your palms flat on the floor, slightly in front of your head. Next, raise your knees and rest them on your elbows. Slowly straighten your back and bring your knees together. Finally, straighten out your legs, and enjoy being upside down.

To write his instructions, Arturo began with a **Prewriting** activity using a flow chart. He thought of the steps he follows when he stands on his head. Then he recorded each step on his flow chart. The chart helped Arturo make sure his instructions would be clear and complete. Part of Arturo's flow chart is shown here. Study what he did.

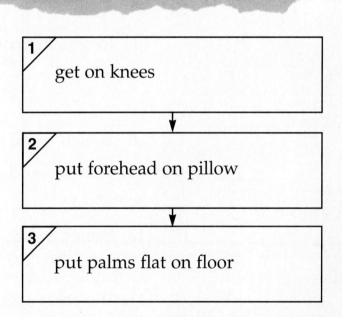

1. get on knees
2. put forehead on pillow
3. put palms flat on floor

Get ready to write your own instructions. You can tell how to make something, how to play a game, or anything you wish. Once you have decided on a topic, make a flow chart. Start at the beginning and be sure to include every important step. Then follow the other steps in the writing process—**Writing, Revising, Proofreading,** and **Publishing.**

Lesson 31 Words with /û/ and /î/

Listen for /û/ and /î/ as you say each word.

third

squirt

dirty

circle

skirt

circus

birth

learn

earn

early

heard

curve

world

germ

★

hear

dear

clear

here

period

cheer

1. Which words begin with a vowel?

_____

2. Which word begins with the letters <u>th</u>?

_____

3. Which word ends with the letters <u>th</u>?

_____

4. Which words begin with the letter <u>d</u>?

_____

5. Which words begin with the letter <u>h</u>?

_____

6. Write the words in which you see the letter <u>c</u> but hear /s/. _____

_____

7. In which word do you see the letter <u>c</u> but hear /k/? _____

_____

8. Which word begins with /j/? _____

9. Which word has the same spelling of /û/ as <u>word</u>? _____

10. Which words end with the same three letters as <u>dirt</u>? _____

11. Which word begins and ends with the same sounds as <u>chair</u>? _____

12. Which word begins and ends like <u>lean</u>?

_____

13. Which word has three syllables?

Checkpoint

Write a spelling word for each clue.
Then use the Checkpoint Study Plan on page 224.

1. The opposite of clean is ___.

2. Today I hear, yesterday I ___.

3. Another word for the universe is the ___.

4. When the flu takes hold, you have a firm ___.

5. not there, but ___

6. not a dress, but a blouse and ___

7. A water pistol is a little ___.

8. The dot at the end of a sentence is a ___.

9. Money you work for is money you ___.

10. The day you were born is the day of your ___.

11. After second comes ___.

12. precious, costly, ___

13. At a football game, give a ___.

14. Box is to ball as square is to ___.

15. not cloudy, but ___

16. The opposite of late is ___.

17. If you can listen, then you can ___.

18. Another word for a bend is a ___.

19. Some people never ___.

20. This mystery word comes from the Greek word *kirkos*. *Kirkos* meant a circle or ring. The Romans changed the spelling of *kirkos* to the spelling we use today. They used this word to describe a large arena with a round stage. Many kinds of athletes performed on this stage. Today this sort of stage is often covered by a tent. Can you guess the mystery word? ___

165

EMMETT KELLY

Weary Willie was a strange clown. He did not have a big smile or funny clothes. Instead, his mouth was set in a downward _____ and his clothes were the _____ rags of a tramp. When he entered the _____ ring, he would chase a _____ of light with a broom and sweep it away. Then he would walk _____ and there, staring sadly into the crowd. People loved Weary Willie. All over the _____, they would _____ loudly for his act.

Inside Weary Willie was a man named Emmett Kelly. His date of _____ was recorded as December 9, 1898. Emmett was not raised in a circus family but grew up on a farm. As a young boy, Emmett was a fine artist. He spent the _____ years of his working life as a cartoonist and drew Weary Willie as a cartoon character. In order to _____ extra money, Emmett would join different circuses and work as a clown.

It didn't take long for Kelly to _____ that he was a great clown. In 1942, he became a member of the Ringling Brothers, Barnum and Bailey Circus. After a short _____ of time, he became their greatest star.

It was not really _____ to Kelly
why everyone loved Weary Willie. Since he never
spoke, people didn't _____ funny jokes
from him! But Weary Willie certainly looked funny,
circling the big top like a gentleman.

Emmett Kelly has told his life story in the book
Clown. Today, Emmett Kelly, Jr., is Weary Willie
and makes people all over the world laugh.

See that funny, painted clown,
A flower in her _____.
Have you heard
Her act is _____,
Her flower sure does _____.
Watch out!
Here comes that funny clown,
Waving, saying, "Hi!"
The crowd will cheer!
"How are you, _____?"
She'll ask and squirt your eye.
Oh, have you _____
Her act is third,
Avoid her like a _____.
And if she tries to squirt your eye,
Don't let her, just stand firm.
Protect yourself from watery clowns,
And the circus will be fun!
But make yourself part of her act,
And you will be undone!

167

third
squirt
dirty
circle
skirt
circus
birth
learn
earn
early
heard
curve
world
germ
hear
dear
clear
here
cheer
period

Plurals and Verb Endings

A dictionary often lists the plural form of a noun when the plural is formed in a special way.

> **cir·cus** | sûr′kəs | *n., pl.* **cir·cus·es.** **1.** A big show put on by acrobats, clowns, and trained animals. **2.** The traveling company that puts on the circus. **3.** A circular arena, surrounded by tiers of seats and often covered by a tent, in which the circus is performed. **4.** An open-air arena used by the ancient Romans for athletic contests and public spectacles. **5.** *Informal.* A place or activity in which there is wild confusion or disorder. **—modifier:** *circus animals.*

1. What is the plural of the word <u>circus</u>? _____

★ Write the following nouns in alphabetical order. Then write the plural form next to each word. Look up each word in the Spelling Dictionary. Only two of these plurals will appear.

baby leaf skirt circle

	Word	Plural
2.		
3.		
4.		
5.		

When the endings <u>ed</u> and <u>ing</u> are added to verbs, the new words are often listed in the entry for the verb.

  Write the following verbs in alphabetical order. Then write the <u>ed</u> and <u>ing</u> forms of each verb.

squirt earn learn cheer clear

	Word	ed	ing
6.			
7.			
8.			
9.			
10.			

Challenge Yourself

courtesy   convert
    worthwhile   interior

Use your Spelling Dictionary to answer these questions. Then write sentences showing that you understand the meaning of each Challenge Word.

1. Would you go outside to see the interior of a building?

2. When you thank someone for a gift, are you showing courtesy?

3. Can you convert a rock into a pool of water or a piece of rock into gold?

4. If you went to a store but found that the store had already closed, was the trip worthwhile?

Write to the Point

The poem on page 167 is about a funny clown. Write a poem about someone. You can write about someone you know or about someone you make up. Tell how this person looks or what he or she likes to wear. You might tell about the person's favorite things to do. Use spelling words from this lesson in your poem.

Challenge Use one or more of the Challenge Words in your poem.

Proofreading

Use the proofreading marks to show the errors in the paragraph below. Write the five misspelled words correctly in the blanks.

At one circas a clown named Dr Sneezo chased a giant jerm in a circle and tried to squrt it with a bottle of green medicine. You could could really here the crowd chear!

	word is misspelled
⊙	period is missing
✄	take out word

1. _____

2. _____

3. _____

4. _____

5. _____

169

Lesson 32 Words with /ə/

Listen for /ə/ as you say each word.

tickle

wrinkle

simple

purple

whistle

wander

winter

chapter

summer

whether

together

special

calendar

blizzard

address

United States
 of America

Canada

dinosaur

automobile

animal

1. Which words begin with a vowel and are not capitalized? _____

_____

2. Which three-syllable words begin with a consonant? _____

_____

_____

3. Which words begin with the letter s?

_____

_____

4. Write the words that begin with /w/ or /hw/.

_____

5. Write the word that begins with the letter w but you don't hear /w/. _____

6. Write the word in which you hear /sh/ but don't see the letters sh. _____

7. Write the word in which /k/ is spelled ck.

_____

8. Write the words that contain double consonants.
dd _____   zz _____
mm _____

9. Which word begins and ends like people?

_____

10. Which words end with ter?

_____

11. Which spelling entry is made up of four words?

Checkpoint

Write a spelling word for each clue.
Then use the Checkpoint Study Plan on page 224.

1. Another word for car is ___.

2. If means ___.

3. A kangaroo is an ___.

4. not apart, but ___

5. Quebec and Toronto are cities in ___.

6. Shower is to hurricane as flurry is to ___.

7. If it is easy, then it is ___.

8. Months, weeks, and days are found on a ___.

9. Page is to paragraph as book is to ___.

10. If I have a line on my face, I have a ___.

11. If you say where you live, you give your ___.

12. fall, winter, spring, and ___

13. The coach blew a ___.

14. After autumn comes ___.

15. not ordinary, but ___

16. The A in U.S.A. means ___.

17. Another word for roam is ___.

18. To touch lightly is to ___.

19. Mix red and blue to get ___.

20. In the early 1800's, a man named Gideon Mantell lived in England. He discovered the fossil tooth of a strange animal. He had never seen such an animal. He tried to think of a name that would describe it. He carefully chose two Greek words: *deinos* and *sauros*. *Deinos* meant terrible. *Sauros* meant lizard. Guess the mystery word, and you'll know whose tooth that was. ___

171

Use each word once to complete these pages.

TRAVELING

On a cold _____ night when I'm in
   my bed,

The wind starts to _____ a song
   in my head.

Outside my window a _____
   is blowing.

I don't even care how hard it is snowing.

I _____ my toes. I
   _____ my nose.

I turn into somebody nobody knows!

The months on the _____
   rush ahead fast,

And I'm in the center of summer at last.

No one is saying, "Tomorrow there's school!"

The water is filling the town swimming pool!

I don't have a test on a _____
   in math,

There are big _____ flowers to pick
   on the path!

I don't need a plane or an _____.

In this make-believe _____, my
   dreams make it real!

On some cold winter night when you're in your
   bed,

Take a trip with the dreams that pass through your
   head!

172

A POSTAL PROBLEM

I'm writing a card to a dinosaur

But I don't know its _____.

If I write, "_____ _____

_____ _____,"

That's not enough, I guess.

Maybe it lives up in _____.

It likes to _____ around.

I'm afraid it won't be _____

For a _____. to be found.

It's such a _____ creature.

No _____ that I know

Is bigger than a dinosaur,

I'd like to watch one grow.

I bought an extra postage stamp

But I still don't know _____

A dinosaur and my small card

Will ever get _____!

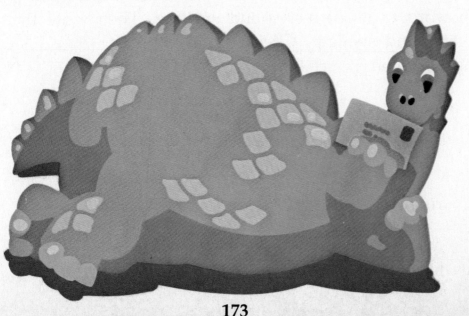

173

tickle
wrinkle
simple
purple
whistle
wander
winter
chapter
summer
whether
together
special
calendar
blizzard
address
United
States of
America
Canada
dinosaur
automobile
animal

Schwa and Accent Marks

The schwa (ə) is a symbol for a certain vowel sound that often occurs in weak, or unstressed, syllables.

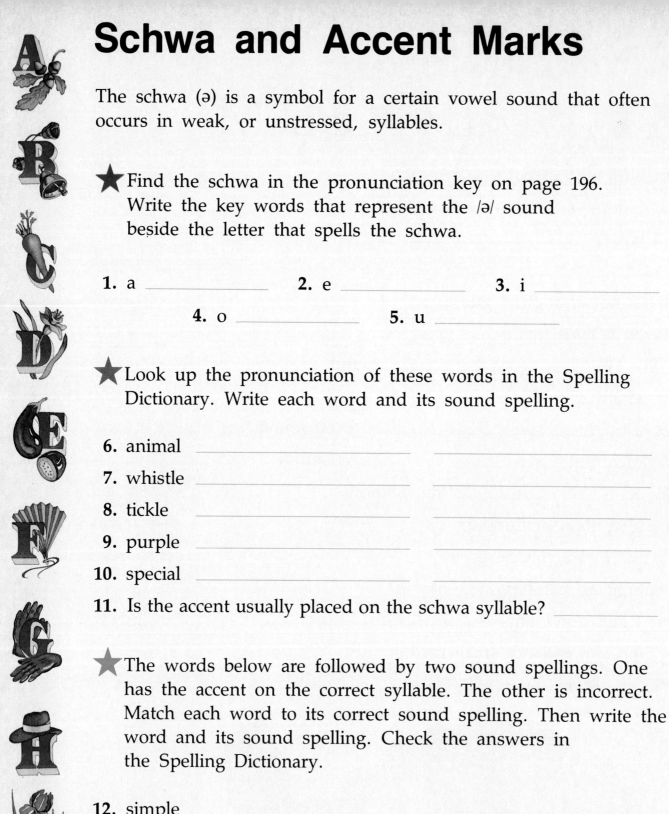

★ Find the schwa in the pronunciation key on page 196. Write the key words that represent the /ə/ sound beside the letter that spells the schwa.

1. a _____   2. e _____   3. i _____

   4. o _____   5. u _____

★ Look up the pronunciation of these words in the Spelling Dictionary. Write each word and its sound spelling.

6. animal _____   _____

7. whistle _____   _____

8. tickle _____   _____

9. purple _____   _____

10. special _____   _____

11. Is the accent usually placed on the schwa syllable? _____

★ The words below are followed by two sound spellings. One has the accent on the correct syllable. The other is incorrect. Match each word to its correct sound spelling. Then write the word and its sound spelling. Check the answers in the Spelling Dictionary.

12. simple
    /**sĭm**' pəl/   /sĭm **pəl**'/   _____

13. wrinkle
    /**rĭng**' kəl/   /rĭng **kəl**'/   _____

14. blizzard
    /**blĭz**' ərd/   /blĭz **ərd**'/   _____

Challenge Yourself

burglar	missile
binoculars	dwindle

Decide which Challenge Word fits each clue. Check your Spelling Dictionary to see if you were right. Then write sentences showing that you understand the meaning of each Challenge Word.

1. Everything looks closer when you look through these.

2. This can be fired at a target that is very far away.

3. Someone who breaks into a house to steal is one of these.

4. Your allowance will do this as you spend it.

Write to the Point

Have you ever been to an interesting place and wished that a friend of yours could have been there, too? The place could be near your home. Or it could be in another city or country. Write a card to your friend telling him or her about this place. Use spelling words from this lesson in your card.

Challenge Use one or more of the Challenge Words in your card.

Proofreading

Use the proofreading marks to show the errors in the paragraph below. Write the five misspelled words correctly in the blanks.

⬭ word is misspelled

⊙ period is missing

≡ letter should be capitalized

I live in Canuda, so a winter trip to florida is a speshal treat for me The calender says it is january, but in Florida it feels like sumer. I can even wandor outdoors without a sweater

1. _____

2. _____

3. _____

4. _____

5. _____

Lesson 33 Compound Words

Say each word.

Solve each compound puzzle.

afternoon	1. after + noon = _____
anything	2. any + thing = _____
forever	3. for + ever = _____
sometimes	4. some + times = _____
without	5. with + out = _____
everybody	6. every + body = _____
basketball	7. basket + ball = _____
countdown	8. count + down = _____
inside	9. in + side = _____
outside	10. out + side = _____
nightmare	11. night + mare = _____
newspaper	12. news + paper = _____
upstairs	13. up + stairs = _____
drugstore	14. drug + store = _____
everywhere	15. every + where = _____
railroad	16. rail + road = _____
weekend	17. week + end = _____
birthday	18. birth + day = _____
downtown	19. down + town = _____
cheeseburger	20. cheese + burger = _____

Checkpoint

Write a spelling word for each clue.
Then use the Checkpoint Study Plan on page 224.

1. What's black and white and read all over? ___.

2. not downstairs, but ___

3. Food is to market as medicine is to ___.

4. Another word for a train line is a ___.

5. Movie is to horror film as dream is to ___.

6. Saturday and Sunday make up the ___.

7. Before a rocket launch, there is a ___.

8. A game with a lot of "hoop-la" is ___.

9. within, or ___

10. a hamburger with melted cheese ___

11. not uptown, but ___

12. in all places ___

13. Always means ___.

14. The opposite of to have is to be ___.

15. Once in a while means ___.

16. Every year, you have a ___.

17. Cowhide is the cow's ___.

18. If I have to, I can do ___.

19. 12:01 P.M. is the start of the ___.

20. Have you ever heard someone called a busybody? A busybody is someone who is busy minding other people's business. In busybody, the word <u>body</u> means the whole person instead of the outward or physical part of a person. The mystery word has the same use of the word <u>body</u>. It means every person. Can you guess the word? ___

177

Use each word once to complete this story.

The Best Weekend of My Life

It was Sunday, April 7, 1978. I remember the date because my tenth _____ was the day before. I was sitting around, not doing much of _____, when my brother, Gus, walked in.

"How would you like to take a ride into Boston with me?" he asked. He pulled out two tickets to the Celtics _____ game. "Happy birthday!"

"I can't believe it!" I screamed. "How did you get those tickets? _____ in Boston wants to see John Havlicek's last game!"

He smiled. "Well, I'd like to say that I got them _____ any trouble, but 'I cannot tell a lie.' It was a _____, waiting _____ the ticket office at the Garden. The crowds were unbelievable!"

I ran _____ to get my jacket and raced out to the _____ station with Gus. We caught the train into _____ Boston and arrived a little after noon. All the stores in the station and even the little _____ were filled with Havlicek buttons. I didn't care much about eating anything, but Gus bought us each a _____ and then we went _____.

The Garden was packed with screaming fans. Banners hung _____. Some said: "Boston loves Hondo." That's Havlicek's nickname. When the speeches were over, Hondo stepped up to the microphone and said, "Thank you, Boston. I love you!" The fans went wild. It seemed as though they stood on their feet and cheered _____.

Then, the game began. Hondo scored 29 points. A few minutes before the game ended, he was pulled and the crowd stood up. It was the end of a 16-year career. In the last seconds of the game, the fans began the _____. The Celtics won, but it was John Havlicek's day. The _____ reported that he turned the lights out in the Garden that night.

Well, I really do think that, with my birthday on Saturday and the Havlicek game on Sunday _____, it was the best _____ of my life.

_____, I wonder if pro basketball will ever see the likes of John Havlicek again.

afternoon
anything
forever
sometimes
without
everybody
basketball
countdown
inside
outside
nightmare
newspaper
upstairs
drugstore
everywhere
railroad
weekend
birthday
downtown
cheeseburger

Capitals

Geographic names such as cities, states, bodies of water, mountains, and streets are capitalized.

Boston   *Swiss Alps*   *Main Street*   *Goose Bay*   *Utah*

★ Capitalize the geographic names in the sentences below. Also correct the misspelled word in each sentence.

1. The Plain Dealer is a noospaper published in cleveland, ohio.

_____

_____

2. The rialroad line was built across rollins street.

_____

_____

★ Read the postcard below. Find the words that are misspelled and the words that need capitals. Write them correctly.

June 25, 199__

Hi Joan,
*   The weather is great here in florida. I have a sunburn, but I still spend time outsid on the beach. This afternun we visited disney World in Orlando. Tomorrow we go to the Everglades.*
*   Your friend forrever,*
*   Ann*

Joan Tomlin
182 Maple avenue
cairo, illinois

3. _____   4. _____

5. _____   6. _____

7. _____   8. _____

9. _____   10. _____

Challenge Yourself

farmland   dewdrops
crossroads   dishwasher

What do you think each underlined Challenge Word means? Check your Spelling Dictionary to see if you are right. Then write sentences showing that you understand the meaning of each Challenge Word.

1. He loaded the dirty plates and cups into the <u>dishwasher</u>.

2. This morning the <u>dewdrops</u> on the grass tickled my bare feet.

3. To make driving safer, the mayor asked that stop signs be placed at the <u>crossroads</u>.

4. <u>Farmland</u> must have good soil for raising crops.

Write to the Point

Do you remember a weekend that was one of the best in your life? Maybe you did something you had always wanted to do. Write a paragraph about what happened that weekend and what made it so special. Or write about something you <u>wish</u> would happen some weekend. Use spelling words from this lesson in your paragraph.

Challenge Use one or more of the Challenge Words in your paragraph.

Proofreading

Use the proofreading marks to show the errors in the paragraph below. Write the five misspelled words correctly in the blanks.

⬭	word is misspelled
≡	letter should be capitalized
⸮∧	question mark is missing

Everbody sang "Happy Birthday" to Jo. Then, Mom ran upstares and brought down a large box witout a top. what do you think jo found enside, asleep on some news paper

1. _____
2. _____
3. _____
4. _____
5. _____

Lesson 34 Abbreviations

in
ft
yd
mi.
c.
pt.
q.
gal.
cm
m.
km
l
F
C
Rte.
Ave.
St.
Blvd.
Rd.
RFD

1. Write the abbreviations for these words.

   inch _____

   foot _____

   yard _____

   mile _____

   centimeter _____

   meter _____

   kilometer _____

   cup _____

   pint _____

   quart _____

   gallon _____

   liter _____

   Fahrenheit _____

   Celsius _____

2. Write the abbreviations that begin with capital letters and end with periods.

   Avenue _____

   Road _____

   Street _____

   Route _____

   Boulevard _____

3. Write the abbreviation with all capital letters and no period.

   Rural Free Delivery _____

Checkpoint

Write a spelling word for each clue.

Unit	Abbreviation		Metric Unit	Abbreviation
1. inches	_____	× 2.5 =	centimeters	_____
2. feet	_____	× 30 =	centimeters	_____
3. yards	_____	× .90 =	meters	_____
4. miles	_____	× 1.6 =	kilometers	_____
5. cups	_____	× .24 =	liters	_____
6. pints	_____	× .47 =	liters	_____
7. quarts	_____	× .95 =	liters	_____
8. gallons	_____	× 3.8 =	liters	_____
9. Fahrenheit	_____	× 5/9 after subtracting 32 = Celsius		_____

10. short for rural free delivery

11. short for road

12. short for boulevard

13. short for avenue

14. short for street

15. short for route

16. This mystery word comes from the Greek word *metron*, which meant a measure or a rule. The Romans spelled it *metrum*, and the French changed it to *metre*. Today the mystery word means about 40 inches. Write the abbreviation for this word.

183

Use the abbreviations from your spelling list to complete these pages.

Rosewood High School has a basketball game at Lakeside School.

The two schools are five _____ or eight _____ apart.

Complete the directions to Lakeside, using the map for information.

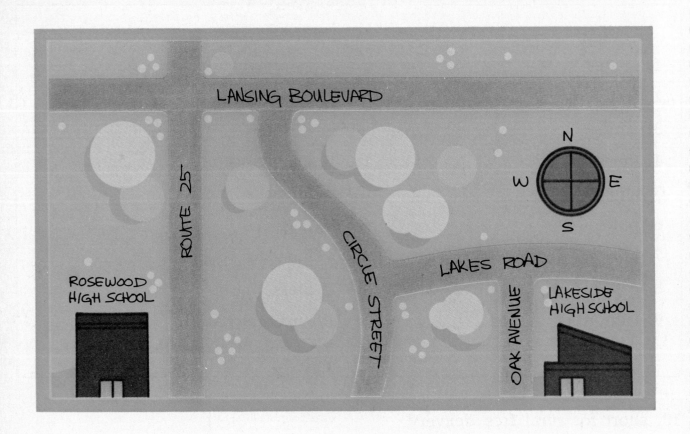

You are traveling north on _____ 25. Turn right onto Lansing _____
Take the first turn off Lansing onto Circle _____ Follow this curving road
until you reach Lakes _____ Turn left. Keep going until you reach
Oak _____ Make a right turn onto Oak. The school is on your left. For
the starting time, write: Lakeside School, _____ 2, Owatonna, Minnesota.

- Rosewood's star player is six _____ six _____ tall.
- At Rosewood players run the hundred-_____ dash for exercise.
- This distance is about the same as ninety _____
- An inch is equal to two and a half _____.

184

RECIPE FOR QUICK WHEATLOAF

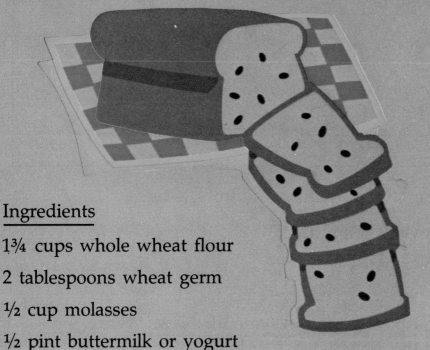

Ingredients

1¾ cups whole wheat flour

2 tablespoons wheat germ

½ cup molasses

½ pint buttermilk or yogurt

½ cup raisins

½ teaspoon baking soda

pinch of salt

Mix 1¾ cups flour with wheat germ, baking soda, and salt. Add ½ _____ molasses and ½ _____ buttermilk to dry ingredients. Stir in raisins. Pour into greased loaf pan and bake at 375° _____ or 190° _____ for 30 minutes.

Serving suggestions:

For 4 people, serve Quick Wheatloaf with a _____ of orange juice or milk. This equals a little more than 1 _____.

For more than 4 people, serve bread with a _____ of apple cider!

185

in
ft
yd
mi.
c.
pt.
q.
gal.
cm
m.
km
l
F
C
Rte.
Ave.
St.
Blvd.
Rd.
RFD

Abbreviations

Abbreviations are used to save time or space.

> Miss Vicki Barsh
> 44 Lincoln St.
> Brookline, MA   02146
>
>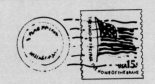
>
>   Mr. and Mrs. Manuel Prestimo
>   1313 Blueview Rd.
>   South Weymouth, MA   02190

 ★ Often, people use abbreviations to address letters.

1. What is the abbreviation for <u>street</u>? _____

2. What is the abbreviation for <u>road</u>? _____

 ★ Vicki wrote this article for the <u>Weymouth News</u>. Write the abbreviations for the underlined words.

> Casey Prestimo was the hero of
> the day when he broke the South High
> record in the 1500-<u>meter</u> race. The   3. _____
> event took place yesterday at Weymouth
> South High School on Pleasant <u>Avenue</u>.   4. _____
> The previous record for the one-and-a-
> half <u>kilometer</u> run was 4:41.   5. _____
>   Casey stays in shape by running
> 6 <u>miles</u> every morning along Union   6. _____
> <u>Boulevard</u>. He also insists that his   7. _____
> diet helps to keep him fit. He drinks
> a <u>quart</u> of milk daily and eats a   8. _____
> <u>pint</u> of yogurt with fresh fruit for lunch. 9. _____

Challenge Yourself

| oz | lb. | g | kg |

Decide which Challenge Word fits each pair of clues. Check your Spelling Dictionary to see if you were right. Then write sentences showing that you understand the meaning of each Challenge Word.

1. I am a little more than two pounds. My name means one thousand grams.

2. I am much less than an ounce. I am used by scientists.

3. I am used by most people in the United States. They use me to tell how much they weigh.

4. There are 16 of me in a pound. I am about the same as 28 grams.

Write to the Point

How good are you at giving directions? Can you tell someone how to get to your school or how to make lemonade? Write a set of directions telling how to go from your home to some other place. Or write directions for preparing a simple snack, such as cereal or chocolate milk. Use abbreviations from this lesson in your directions.

Challenge Use one or more of the Challenge Words in your directions.

Proofreading

Use the proofreading marks to show the errors in the paragraph below. Write the five misspelled words correctly in the blanks.

At the corner of Shady Str. and third Av., turn left and go about fifty f down the block. go past Allen Rd Turn right onto Rt. 7. The library is one mle. down the road.

⬭	word is misspelled
⊙	period is missing
≡	letter should be capitalized

1. _____

2. _____

3. _____

4. _____

5. _____

Lesson 35 The Universe

Say each word.

Mercury
Venus
Earth
Mars
Jupiter
Saturn
Uranus
Neptune
Pluto
solar system
galaxy
universe
satellite
comet
meteor
constellation
planets
rotate
revolve
gravity

1. Write the words that begin with capital letters.

_____   _____

_____   _____

_____   _____

2. Write the word that begins with a vowel and does not have a capital letter.

_____

3. Which words begin with /k/?

_____

4. Which words begin with the letter r?

5. Which words begin with the letter g?

_____

6. Write the words that have double consonants.
   ll _____
   ll _____

7. Write the three-syllable word that begins with the letter m and does not have a capital letter.

_____

8. Write the entry that is made up of two words.

_____

9. Solve this:

planet + s = _____

Checkpoint

Write a spelling word for each clue.
Then use the Checkpoint Study Plan on page 224.

1. Paint is to picture as stars are to ___.

2. We live on this sun-orbiting body. ___

3. It keeps your feet on the ground. ___

4. Nine of them orbit the sun. ___

5. "the red planet"; fourth from the sun ___

6. To spin around something is to ___.

7. the largest planet in our solar system ___

8. a shooting star ___

9. the planet named for the King of the Sea ___

10. the planet named for the goddess of love ___

11. the sun, the nine planets, and their satellites ___

12. Flame is to match as tail is to ___.

13. The seventh planet is ___.

14. ninth planet discovered in this solar system ___

15. Tops are to spin as planets are to ___.

16. Another word for moon is ___.

17. The planet with rings is ___.

18. All existing things are in the ___.

19. The sun's closest neighbor is ___.

20. This mystery word means a large collection of stars. Does it surprise you that it comes from a word that means milk? It comes from *galactos*, the Greek word for milk. This is because a collection of stars in the sky looks white like milk. In fact, the collection of stars in which we live is called the Milky Way. Can you guess the mystery word? ___

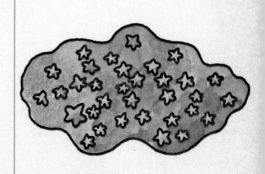

189

The Universe

The Earth is just one tiny part of the great

_____. All around us in space

are millions of other _____ and

stars. We are part of a _____, or

family of stars, called the Milky Way. Our sun is

only one of the stars that make up the Milky Way.

Our sun and all the things that move around it

are called the _____ _____.

The sun has enough _____, or

pull, to keep our solar system in order. Nine

planets _____ around the sun.

As they move, the planets also spin around, or

_____. Some planets have small

objects that revolve around them! They are called

moons or satellites. The Earth has only one

_____ while Jupiter has 13!

The four planets nearest the sun are

_____, _____,

_____, and _____. They are

made up of mostly iron and rock. The next four

bodies are _____,

_____, _____, and

_____. They seem to be made up

chiefly of gases. _____ is the farthest

planet from the sun. Too little is known about Pluto

to place it in either group.

There are many other interesting parts of the

universe. Star watchers like to pick out groups of

stars. A _____, called

the Big Dipper, is a favorite. Others enjoy spotting

a shooting star, or _____, blazing

through the sky. Some people study the bright tail

of a _____.

The universe holds many secrets. As we send off

each new space capsule, we come a little closer to

understanding what lies out there in space!

191

Mercury
Venus
Earth
Mars
Jupiter
Saturn
Uranus
Neptune
Pluto
solar system
galaxy
universe
satellite
comet
meteor
constellation
planets
rotate
revolve
gravity

Colons

Use a colon (:) after a word that introduces a series or list.

Aunt Mary prepared my favorite dinner: roast beef, mashed potatoes, broccoli, and apple pie.

★ Write each sentence below. Place a colon after the word that introduces the list in each sentence.

1. There are four terrestrial or earth-like planets in our solar system Mercury, Venus, Earth, and Mars. _____

_____

_____

2. There is little earth-like substance on the next four planets Jupiter, Saturn, Uranus, and Neptune. _____

_____

_____

3. Those planets are made up of gases hydrogen, helium, ammonia, and methane. _____

_____

4. The universe holds many wonders constellations, comets, meteors, and asteroids. _____

_____

_____

5. On a clear night I can spot four constellations the Big Dipper, Orion, the Little Dipper, and Gemini. _____

_____

_____

Challenge Yourself

physics   vastness
        takeoff   technology

Use your Spelling Dictionary to answer these questions. Then write sentences showing that you understand the meaning of each Challenge Word.

1. Is it important to understand <u>physics</u> before you start to build a spaceship?

2. Can we explore the <u>vastness</u> of outer space in one day?

3. If a rocket is ready for <u>takeoff</u>, is it ready to land?

4. Without <u>technology</u>, could people walk on the moon?

Write to the Point

Technology has led to inventions like jets, telephones, and space shuttles. Imagine that you could invent a machine or a way to travel. Write a description of your invention and explain how it would help people. Use spelling words from this lesson in your description.

Challenge Use one or more of the Challenge Words in your description.

Proofreading

Use the proofreading marks to show the errors in the paragraph below. Write the five misspelled words correctly in the blanks.

◯	word is misspelled
≡	letter should be capitalized
∧	word is missing

After leaving Erth, Captain diego stopped on Mercurie, venus, and Marrs. Once, a metiore almost hit the spaceship. When we last heard from him, he heading for Pluto, at the far edge of our solor systum.

1. _____

2. _____

3. _____

4. _____

5. _____

Lesson 36 Words in Review

A. circle
heard
curve
germ
world

B. clear
cheer
here
period

C. special
simple
together
animal
automobile

D. basketball

E. c.
pt.
gal.
C
F

★**Use a piece of paper for the starred activities.**

1. In Lesson 31 you studied five ways to spell /û/: i, ea, u, o, e. Write the words in list A. _____

   _____

   _____

2. You also studied three ways to spell /î/: ea, e, ee. Write the words in list B.

   _____ _____

   _____ _____

3. In Lesson 32 you studied four ways to spell /ə/: e, a, o, i. Write the words in list C.

   _____ _____

   _____ _____

★4. Write the words in lists A, B, and C. Look up each in the Spelling Dictionary and write the sound spelling beside each word.

5. In Lesson 33 you studied compounds. Write the compound review word. _____

★6. Write two sentences about the word <u>basketball</u>.

7. In Lesson 34 you studied abbreviations. Write the abbreviations for the following words:

   cup_____   gallon_____   Fahrenheit_____

   pint_____   Celsius_____

★8. Write a recipe using three abbreviations listed above.

Writer's Workshop

A Description

A description of a person is sometimes called a character sketch. In a character sketch, the writer describes how a person looks and how he or she acts. The writer usually pays close attention to the things that stand out most about the person. Here is the beginning of Sheila's description of her sister Denise. What things stand out most about Sheila's sister?

My Sister

My sister Denise is eleven years old, but people usually think she is older because she is very tall for her age. She has short black hair that she always holds back with a red headband. She likes to wear my brother's old sweatshirts.

Denise is a very cheerful person. She is always smiling and laughing, and she makes other people laugh.

To write her description, Sheila followed the steps in the writing process. She began with a **Prewriting** activity using a list. Making the list helped Sheila recall some exact details that she could use to describe her sister. Then she chose the best ones to use in her description. Part of Sheila's list is shown here. Study what Sheila did.

My sister Denise
how she looks
    tall
    short black hair
    wears sweatshirts
    long fingernails
how she acts
    cheerful
    smiles and laughs
    friendly

Get ready to write your own description of a person. You can write about someone in your neighborhood or anyone you wish. Make a list of exact details about how that person looks and acts. Choose the ones you think will interest your reader. Then follow the other steps in the writing process—**Writing, Revising, Proofreading,** and **Publishing.**

SPELLING
Dic·tion·ar·y

A

a•bove | ə **bŭv′** | *adv.* In a higher place: *the sun above.* —*prep.* Over; higher than.

ab•sence | **ăb′** səns | *n.* **1.** The condition of not being present: *The absence of snow was unusual.* **2.** The condition of being away: *Your absence from school was noticed.*

ac•cuse | ə **kyōōz′** | *v.* **ac•cused, ac•cus•ing.** To blame someone for doing something wrong: *Mark accused him of breaking his bat.*

ac•knowl•edge | ăk **nŏl′** ĭj | *v.* **ac•knowl•edged, ac•knowl•edg•ing.** To admit as true or as existing: *I acknowledge that I was wrong.*

ac•quaint | ə **kwānt′** | *v.* **acquaint•ed, ac•quaint•ing.** To make or become familiar: *I must acquaint myself with the rules of the game.*

ac•quire | ə **kwīr′** | *v.* **ac•quired, ac•quir•ing.** To get or gain: *How did you acquire the baseball card?*

ac•ro•bat | **ăk′** rə băt′ | *n.* A person who is

skilled in performing daring actions such as swinging on a trapeze or walking a tightrope.

ad•dress | ə **drĕs′** | *n.* **1.** *also* | **ăd′** rĕs | Place where a person lives, works, or gets mail. **2.** A speech: *State of the Union Address.* —*v.* **1.** To write on mail where it should go. **2.** To speak to: *address a crowd.*

a•dorn | ə **dôrn′** | *v.* To decorate in order to make beautiful: *Norma wanted to adorn the package with a bow.*

a•fraid | ə **frād′** | *adj.* **1.** Fearful; frightened: *afraid of high places.* **2.** Sorry to say: *I'm afraid you're right.*

af•ter•noon |ăf′ tər **nōōn′** | *or* |äf′- | *n.* The part of the day between noon and sunset.

a•gain | ə **gĕn′** | *adv.* **1.** Once more: *Let me try again.* **2.** On the other hand: *It may snow and then again it may not.*

a•gainst | ə **gĕnst′** | *prep.* **1.** In a position opposite to: *against the rules.* **2.** So as to meet: *He hit the ball against the wall.*

air | âr | *n.* **1.** A mixture of gases surrounding the earth. **2.** Space overhead.

air•borne | **âr′** bôrn′ | *or* | **âr′** bōrn′ | *adj.* **1.** Carried by or through the air: *The wind made the leaf airborne.* **2.** Flying: *The plane is airborne high in the sky.*

a•larm | ə lärm | *n.* **1.** Sudden fear of danger: *cause for alarm.* **2.** A signal to warn people: *a fire alarm.* —*v.* To frighten.

al•most | **ôl′** mōst | *or* | ôl **mōst′** | *adv.* Just about; nearly: *The pie is almost ready.*

a•lone | ə **lōn′** | *adj.* Without the company of other people or things. —*adv.* Without help: *I cooked dinner alone.*

al•read•y | ôl **rĕd′** ē | *adj.* By this time: *The book is already overdue.*

a•mong | ə **mŭng′** | *prep.* **1.** One of: *Monkeys are among the best-loved animals.* **2.** In the company of: *among relatives.* **3.** With portions to each: *divided among us.*

an•gry | **ăng′** grē | *adj.* **an•gri•er, an•gri•est.** Feeling or showing anger: *an angry neighbor; an angry look.*

an•i•mal | **ăn′** ə məl | *n.* A living thing differing from a plant by its ability to move about, grow to a limited size and shape, and feed upon other animals or plants.

an•oth•er | ə **nŭth′** ər | *adj.* **1.** Different: *another way to go.* **2.** One more: *another piece of pie.*

an•swer | **ăn′** sər | *or* | **än′** - | *n.* **1.** A spoken or written response to a question. **2.** Solution to a problem. —*v.* To reply.

an•y•thing | **ĕn′** ē thĭng′ | *pron.* Any object, event, or subject whatever.

a•part | ə **pärt′** | *adv.* **1.** Separate in time or distance: *miles apart.* **2.** In pieces: *The toy fell apart.*

ap•plaud | ə **plôd′** | *v.* To clap hands to show approval: *The Senate applauded the President's speech.*

ap•point | ə **point′** | *v.* To name or choose for a duty or position: *The teacher appointed the class helpers.*

ap•pro•pri•ate | ə **prō′** prē ĭt | *adj.* Right; proper: *Games are appropriate gifts for a ten-year-old.*

a•pri•cot | **ăp′** rĭ kŏt′ | *or* | **ā′** prĭ kŏt′ | *n.* A juicy, round, yellowish-orange fruit that looks like a peach: *The apricot in the lunchbox was for dessert.*

A•pril | **ā′** prəl | *n.* The fourth month of the year.

aren't | ärnt | *or* | **är′** ənt |. **1.** Are not. **2.** Am not (in questions).

ask | ăsk | *or* | äsk | *v.* **asked, ask•ing. 1.** To question: *She asked him about his house.* **2.** Request: *Ask him to sing!* **3.** Invite: *She asked them to dinner.*

at•tor•ney | ə **tŭr′** nē | *n., pl.* **at•tor•neys.** A lawyer: *The attorney gave me advice about the law.*

auc•tion | **ôk′** shən | *n.* A public sale at which things are sold to the people who offer the most money: *The movie star's car will be sold at an auction.* —*v.* To sell at an auction: *The museum will auction the painting.*

au•di•o | **ô′** dē ō′ | *adj.* Having to do with sound or how it is recorded, played, or received: *The school needs new audio equipment to make the band's concerts sound better.*

Au•gust | **ô′** gəst | *n.* The eighth month of the year.

aunt | ănt | *or* | änt | *n.* **1.** The sister of one's father or mother. **2.** The wife of one's uncle.

au•thor | ô′ thər | *n.* A person who writes books, stories, etc.

au•to•mo•bile | ô′ tə mə **bēl′** | *or* |-**mō′** bēl′ | *or* | **ô′** tə mə bēl′ | *n.* A passenger vehicle for use on land. It carries its own engine and moves on four wheels.

au•tumn | ô′ təm | *n.* The season of the year between summer and winter; fall.

Ave. Avenue.

a•void | ə **void′** | *v.* **1.** To keep away from: *avoid traffic.* **2.** To prevent: *Dress warmly to avoid catching cold.*

a•wake | ə **wāk′** | *v.* **a•woke** | ə **wōk′** |, **a•waked, a•wak•ing.** To rise from sleep. —*adj.* Not asleep: *He was wide awake.*

awe•some | ô′ səm | *adj.* Causing wonder, respect, or fear: *The Grand Canyon is an awesome sight.*

a•while | ə **hwīl′** | *or* | ə **wīl′** | *adv.* For a short time: *They sat awhile.*

ax•le | **ăk′** səl | *n.* A bar on which a wheel or set of wheels turns: *The car axle broke when the wheels hit a big hole in the road.*

B

ba•by | **bā′** bē | *n., pl.* **ba•bies. 1.** A very young child; infant. **2.** The youngest in a group or family.

bal•loon | bə **loon′** | *n.* **1.** Airtight bag filled with gas that is lighter than air so that it will float. **2.** A child's toy made of rubber, filled with air.

ba•nan•a | bə **năn′** ə | *n.* A crescent-shaped tropical fruit that is sweet, soft, and yellow-skinned.

ban•ish | **băn′** ĭsh | *v.* **ban•ished, ban•ish•ing, ban•ish•es. 1.** To force to leave a country or place: *The king will banish the robbers.* **2.** To drive away: *Tim will banish his fears by singing.*

bar•ri•er | **băr′** ē ər | *n.* Something that blocks the way or blocks movement: *The tree that fell on the road was a barrier.*

bas•ket•ball | **băs′** kĭt bôl′ | *or* | **bä′** skĭt- | *n.* **1.** A game played by two teams. Players

toss a ball through a basket defended by other team. **2.** The ball used in this game.

beach | bēch | *n.* The shore beside a body of water.

bea•con | **bē′** kən | *n.* A light or other type of signal that guides or warns: *The beacon helped the plane to land.*

beau•ti•ful | **byoo′** tə fəl | *adj.* Having beauty; pleasing to see or hear: *the beautiful gem.*

be•cause | bĭ **kôz′** | *or* | -**kŭz′** | *conj.* For the reason that: *He went to bed because he was tired.*

be•come | bĭ **kŭm′** | *v.* **be•came** | bĭ **kām′** |, **be•come, be•com•ing.** To grow to be: *She becomes restless during long speeches.*

be•fore | bĭ **fôr′** | *or* | -**fōr′** | *adv.* Earlier: *I've been here before.* —*prep.* In front of: *She stood before the judge.*

be•gan | bĭ **găn′** |. Look up **begin.**

be•gin | bĭ **gĭn′** | *v.* **be•gan** | bĭ **găn′** |, **be•gun** | bĭ **gŭn′** |, **be•gin•ning. 1.** To start. **2.** Come or bring into being: *The storm began an hour ago.*

be•hind | bĭ **hīnd′** | *prep.* In back of: *He hid behind the chair.*

be•low | bĭ **lō′** | *adv.* Lower than; under: *The playroom is below the living room.*

be•side | bĭ **sīd′** | *prep.* At the side of: *The house stood beside the lake.*

be•tray | bĭ **trā′** | *v.* **1.** To help the enemy of: *The man would not betray his country and become a spy for its enemy.* **2.** To be disloyal to: *I promised not to betray my friend by telling his secret to anyone.*

be•tween | bĭ **twēn′** | *prep.* In the time or space separating two things: *The river runs between Minnesota and North Dakota.*

be•yond | bē **ŏnd′** | *or* | bĭ **yŏnd′** | *prep.* **1.** On the farther side of: *His paper route goes beyond the school.* **2.** Later than; after: *He stayed beyond midnight to complete his work.*

bin•oc•u•lars | bə **nŏk′** yə lərz | *pl. n.* A device consisting of two small telescopes joined together that makes distant objects look closer and larger: *We used binoculars to see the eagle's nest.*

birth | bûrth | *n.* The beginning of one's existence: *the birth of the baby.*

birth•day | **bûrth′** dā′ | *n.* **1.** The day on which a person is born. **2.** The yearly return of that day.

blind | blīnd | *adj.* **1.** Unable to see: *a blind person.* **2.** Hidden: *a blind curve.* —*v.* To make unable to see: *The bright light blinded him.*

bliz•zard | **blĭz′** ərd | *n.* A heavy snowstorm with strong winds.

blood | blŭd | *n.* Red liquid circulated through the body by the heart, carrying oxygen and food to body parts.

blouse | blous | *or* | blouz | *n.* A loose shirtlike piece of clothing for the part of the body from the neck to waist: *Ling wore a blue blouse.*

Blvd. Boulevard.

bod•y | **bŏd′** ē | *n., pl.* **bod•ies.** The whole physical structure of a living thing: *I jog to keep my body in shape.*

book•store | **bŏŏk′** stôr′ | *or* | **bŏŏk′** stōr′ | *n.* A store that sells books: *I can spend hours in a bookstore because I love to buy and read books.*

boost | bōŏst | *n.* A shove or push upward: *Give me a boost over the wall.* —*v.* To lift or push up.

bot•tom | **bŏt′** əm | *n.* The lowest part of anything: *the bottom of the barrel.*

bought | bôt |. Look up **buy.**

bou•quet | bō **kā′** | *or* | bōō **kā′** | *n.* A number of flowers grouped together:

The bouquet of yellow roses was beautiful.

bowl¹ | bōl | *n.* A hollow, round dish used for holding food, flowers, etc.

bowl² | bōl | *v.* To play a game of bowling.

box | bŏks | *n., pl.* **box•es.** A container having four sides, a bottom, and a lid.

branch | brănch | *or* | bränch | *n., pl.* **branch•es.** Woody stem growing out from the trunk of a tree.

bread | brĕd | *n.* Food made from moistened flour, then leavened, kneaded, and baked.

break | brāk | *v.* **broke** | brōk |, **bro•ken** | **brō′** kən |, **break•ing. 1.** To come apart; split into fragments. **2.** To make unusable: *Billy broke my radio.*

break•fast | **brĕk′** fəst | *n.* The first meal of the day: *It is important to eat a good breakfast.*

bridge | brĭj | *n.* A structure built over a river, railroad, or other obstacle providing a way across.

bright | brīt | *adj.* **bright•er, bright•est. 1.** Giving off light in large amounts: *the bright sun.* **2.** Smart: *the bright child.*

bring | brĭng | *v.* **brought** | brôt |, **bring•ing.** To carry along: *Bring some pajamas with you!*

broke | brōk |. Look up **break.**

brook | brŏŏk | *n.* A small freshwater stream.

broth•er | **brŭ*th*′** ər | *n., pl.* **broth•ers.** A boy or man whose parents are the same as another person's.

brought | brôt |. Look up **bring.**

brush | brŭsh | *n., pl.* **brush•es.** A tool with bristles used for cleaning, painting, grooming, etc. —*v.* **1.** To clean, paint, or groom with a brush. **2.** To touch in passing.

build | bĭld | *v.* **built** | bĭlt |, **build•ing. 1.** To make by fitting together: *build a house.* **2.** To create by process or plan: *to build strong bodies.*

build•ing | **bĭl′** dĭng | *n.* **1.** Something that's built: *an apartment building.* **2.** Process of constructing.

bur•glar | **bûr′** glər | *n., pl.* **bur•glars.** A person who breaks into a house, store, or other building to steal something: *The burglar who had broken into the store and stolen money was caught by the police.*

bus | bŭs | *n., pl.* **bus•es** or **bus•ses.** A large motor vehicle equipped to carry many passengers.

bush | bŏŏsh | *n.* A small, woody, branching plant: *I love the smell of lilac bushes!*

bus•y | **bĭz′** ē | *adj.* **bus•i•er, bus•i•est.** Having a lot to do; active: *the busy secretary.*

but•ton | **bŭt′** n | *n.* A small disk sewn to clothes to hold them closed or decorate them.

buy | bī | *v.* **bought** | bôt |, **bought, buy•ing.** To get in exchange for money; purchase: *I would love to buy that rolltop desk.*

C

C Celsius.

c. cup.

cal•en•dar | **kăl′** ən dər | *n.* A table showing time by days, weeks, months, and years.

can | kăn| *or* | kən | *v.* Able to do or accomplish: *I can ride a bike.*

Can•a•da | **kăn′** ə də |. A country in North America, extending from the Atlantic to the Pacific and from the U.S. to the Arctic Ocean.

care•ful | **kâr′** fəl | *adj.* **1.** Taking care; watchful. **2.** Done with care.

car•ry | **kăr′** ē | *v.* **car•ried, car•ry•ing.** To bear in your hands or on your back while moving.

car•toon | kär **tōōn′** | *n.* **1.** A drawing showing people, things, or events in a humorous way. **2.** Comic strip. **3.** Animated film.

catch | kăch | *v.* **caught** | kôt |, **catch•ing. 1.** To grab hold of: *catch the ball.* **2.** To trap: *We set traps to catch the mice.*

caught | kôt |. Look up **catch.**

cause | kôz | *n.* **1.** Person or thing that makes something happen. **2.** Reason for action. **3.** A goal: *the cause of freedom.* —*v.* **caused, caus•ing.** To make happen: *Carelessness caused the fire!*

change | chānj | *v.* **changed, chang•ing. 1.** Make or become different. **2.** Put in place of another. **3.** To exchange.

chap•ter | **chăp′** tər | *n.* A main division of a book: *the chapter on trout fishing.*

chase | chās | *v.* **chased, chas•ing. 1.** To run after or follow in order to catch. **2.** To drive away.

cheer | chîr | *v.* **1.** To shout in praise. **2.** To give support: *The team cheered her on!*

cheese•burg•er | **chēz′** bûr′ gər | *n.* A hamburger topped with melted cheese.

chick•en | **chĭk′** ən | *or* | -ĭn | *n.* Domestic fowl raised for food; hen or rooster.

child | chīld | *n., pl.* **chil•dren** | **chĭl′** drən |. **1.** A young boy or girl. **2.** A son or daughter. **child's** —*poss.* Belonging to the child. **chil•dren's** —*poss.* Belonging to the children.

choice | chois | *n.* **1.** The act of choosing or selecting. **2.** A person or thing chosen.

choose | chōōz | *v.* **chose** | chōz |, **cho•sen** | **chō′** zən |, **choos•ing. 1.** Select from a number; pick out. **2.** Decide: *He chose to stay inside.*

cho•rus | **kôr′** əs | *or* | **kōr′** - | *n., pl.* **cho•rus•es. 1.** A group of singers who perform together. **2.** A musical composition written for a group.

chose | chōz |. Look up **choose.**

cir•cle | **sûr′** kəl | *n.* A closed curve that has points equally distant from its fixed center.

cir•cus | **sûr′** kəs | *n., pl.* **cir•cus•es.** A show with acrobats, clowns, and trained animals.

cit•y | **sĭt′** ē | *n., pl.* **cit•ies.** A center of people, business, and culture; an important town.

class | klăs | *or* | kläs | *n., pl.* **class•es. 1.** A set of people or things alike in some way. **2.** A group of students learning together.

cleanse | klĕnz | *v.* **cleansed, cleans•ing.** To make clean: *The doctor will cleanse the cut on my hand.*

clear | klîr | *adj.* **clear•er, clear•est. 1.** Free from haze, mist, clouds. **2.** Easily seen, heard, or understood. **3.** Plain, evident.

climb | klīm | *v.* **1.** To go up by using hands or feet. **2.** To rise.

close | klōs | *adj.* **clos•er, clos•est.** Near; together in time or space. —*v.* | klōz | **closed, clos•ing.** To shut: *Close the door.*

clothes | klōz | *or* | klō*th*z | *pl. n.* Coverings for a person's body.

cloud | kloud | *n.* **1.** Mass of water droplets or ice particles in the air. **cloud's** —*poss.* Belonging to the cloud.

cm centimeter.

coach | kōch | *n.* **1.** A large carriage pulled by horses. **2.** Railroad passenger car. **3.** Person who trains athletic teams.

coast | kōst | *n.* The land along the sea. —*v.* To move without the use of power.

cof•fee | **kô′** fē | *or* | **kŏf′** ē | *n.* **1.** A brown

drink made from ground, roasted seeds of a tropical tree. **2.** The seeds of this tree.

coin | koin | *n.* A piece of flat metal stamped by the government to be used as money.

col•lage | kə **läzh′** | *n.* A picture made by pasting different kinds of materials or objects on a surface: *I made a collage of newspaper, yarn, and bottle caps for my art project.*

col•lide | kə **līd′** | *v.* **col•lid•ed, col•lid•ing.** To crash against each other with force: *We saw the cars collide on the highway.*

comb | kōm | *n.* A piece of metal, plastic, etc. with teeth used to arrange or fasten hair. —*v.* **1.** To arrange with a comb. **2.** To search.

com•et | **kŏm′** ĭt | *n.* A bright, celestial mass of material with a starlike center and a tail of light.

con•ceal | kən **sēl′** | *v.* To keep someone or something out of sight or unknown; hide: *He tried to conceal his anger.*

con•stel•la•tion | kŏn′ stə **lā′** shən | *n.* A group of stars having a recognized shape: *The Big Dipper is a familiar constellation.*

con•struct | kən **strŭkt′** | *v.* To build by putting parts together: *The class will construct a model airport.*

con•test | **kŏn′** tĕst′ | *n.* **1.** A fight or struggle to gain victory or superiority. **2.** A competition rated by judges: *an ice-skating contest.*

con•trib•ute | kən **trĭb′** yōōt | *v.* **con•trib•ut•ed, con•trib•ut•ing.** To give to a common cause or purpose: *Tom contributed money to help the flood victims.*

con•vert | kən **vŭrt′** | *v.* **con•vert•ed, con•vert•ing.** To change a thing into something different or into another form: *convert snow into water.*

cook | kŏok | v. **cooked, cook•ing.** To prepare food by using heat.

cop•y | **kŏp′** ē | n., pl. **cop•ies. 1.** A thing made to be exactly like another. **2.** An example of something. —v. **cop•ied, cop•y•ing.** Follow as a model; imitate.

cot•ton | **kŏt′** n | n. **1.** A plant with soft, white fibers surrounding the seeds. **2.** Cloth made from these fibers.

cou•gar | **kōo′**gər | n. A large brown cat. Also called mountain lion.

could | kŏod | or | kəd when unstressed |. Look up **can.**

could•n't | **kŏod′** nt |. Could not.

coun•sel•or | **koun′** sə lər | n. A person who gives advice or helps: a school counselor.

count•down | **kount′** doun′ | n. The process of counting time backward until the time a special event is to take place.

count•er | **koun′** tər | n. A narrow table on which money is counted, or food is served.

coun•try | **kŭn′** trē | n., pl. **coun•tries. 1.** A nation. **2.** Land; region: rough, rocky country.

coun•try•side | **kŭn′** trē sīd′ | n. The region outside towns and cities: The pictures of the countryside are different from the ones of the city.

cou•ple | **kŭp′** əl | n. **1.** Two things of the same kind. **2.** A man and woman who are married; partners. **3.** A few; several.

cou•pon | **kōo′**pŏn | or | **kyōo′**pŏn | n. A ticket or form that can be exchanged to save money or to get something: I had a coupon for the movie.

cour•te•sy | **kûr′** tĭ sē | n., pl. **cour•te•sies.** Behavior that shows good manners and thoughtfulness; politeness: It is a courtesy to say thank you for a gift.

cov•er | **kŭv′** ər | v. **1.** To place something over. **2.** To occupy the surface of.

crack | krăk | v. To break with a sudden noise; split. —n. **1.** A sharp, snapping sound. **2.** A narrow space.

crawl | krôl | v. To move slowly by dragging oneself.

cross•roads | **krŏs′** rōds′ | n. (used with a singular verb). A place where two or more roads meet or cross, often in the countryside: The crossroads is a busy place.

crowd | kroud | n. **1.** A large number of people together. **2.** People in general. —adj. **crowd•ed.** Filled to excess; packed.

crown | kroun | n. **1.** A head covering of metal and jewels worn by a king or queen. **2.** The royal power.

cry | krī | v. **cried, cry•ing, cries. 1.** To shed tears; weep. **2.** A loud call or shout.

curve | kûrv | n. A line that has no straight part but is smooth and continuous.

cus•tom•ar•y | **kŭs′** tə mĕr′ ē | adj. Commonly done; usual: It is customary to eat dessert last.

D

daugh•ter | **dô′** tər | n. A female child or offspring.

dawn | dôn | n. The beginning of day; first appearance of daylight.

deaf•en | **dĕf′** ən | v. To make unable to hear: Music played too loudly can deafen a person.

dear | dîr | adj. **dear•er, dear•est.** Loved; precious: my dear sister. These sound alike **dear, deer.**

De•cem•ber | dĭ **sĕm′** bər | n. The twelfth month of the year.

de•fi•ant | dĭ **fī′** ənt | adj. Showing that one will not obey or respect something or someone in control: The defiant child would not go to bed.

de•liv•er | dĭ **lĭv′** ər | *v.* To carry or take to a person to whom something is addressed: *deliver mail.*

de•ny | dĭ **nī′** | *v.* **de•nied, de•ny•ing, de•nies.** To declare something untrue: *deny a rumor.*

des•ert[1] | **dĕz′** ərt | *n.* A dry region that is sandy and without trees.

de•sert[2] | dĭ **zûrt′** | *v.* To leave: *desert the sinking ship.*

de•stroy | dĭ **stroi′** | *v.* **1.** To ruin or spoil; make useless: *The storm destroyed the house.* **2.** To put an end to: *destroyed her dream.*

dew•drop | **doo′** drŏp′ | *or* | **dyoo′** drŏp′ | *n., pl.* **dew•drops.** A drop of water from the air that collects on cool surfaces, usually at night: *The dewdrops sparkled in the grass.*

did•n't | **dĭd′** nt|. Did not.

die | dī | *v.* **died, dy•ing. 1.** To stop living. **2.** To lose strength: *The wind died down. These sound alike* **die, dye.**

dif•fer•ent | **dĭf′** ər ənt | *or* | **dĭf′** rənt | *adj.* **1.** Not alike: *A car is different from a plane.* **2.** Separate: *three different men.*

dig•ni•fy | **dĭg′** nə fī′ | *v.* **dig•ni•fied, dig•ni•fy•ing, dig•ni•fies.** To give honor to: *It was kind of the teacher to dignify his question with a long answer.*

di•no•saur | **dī′** nə sôr′ | *n.* Any one of a group of extinct reptiles that inhabited the earth millions of years ago.

dirt•y | **dûr′** tē | *adj.* **dirt•i•er, dirt•i•est.** Not clean; soiled: *dirty laundry.*

dis•cov•er | dĭ **skŭv′** ər | *v.* To find out through study or observation: *discover a new medicine.*

dish | dĭsh | *n., pl.* **dish•es. 1.** A flat container for serving food. **2.** Food served: *Ice cream is a tasty dish.*

dish•wash•er | **dĭsh′** wŏsh′ ər | *or* | **dĭsh′** wô′ shər | *n.* **1.** A machine that is used for washing dishes: *A dishwasher makes it easier to clean up after a meal.* **2.** A person who washes dishes.

dis•mal | **dĭz′** məl | *adj.* Causing, feeling, or showing sadness or gloom: *The cold, rainy day was dismal.*

dis•pose | dĭ **spōz′** | *v.* **dis•posed, dis•pos•ing.** To arrange. *Idiom.* **dispose of. 1.** To settle. **2.** To get rid of.

doc•tor | **dŏk′** tər | *n.* A person trained and licensed to practice medicine.

does | dŭz |. Third person form of **do.**

does•n't | **dŭz′** ənt |. Does not.

dol•lar | **dŏl′** ər | *n.* Basic unit of money in the U.S. and Canada, equal to 100 cents.

done | dŭn |. Past participle of **do.** —*adj.* **1.** Finished or completed: *Her work is done.* **2.** Cooked: *well-done meat.*

don't | dōnt |. Do not.

dou•ble | **dub′** əl | *adj.* **1.** Twice as much as: *double the size of.* **2.** Made up of two like parts: *a double dresser.*

down•town | **doun′** toun′ | *adv.* The center or main business section of a city.

Dr. Doctor.

drap•er•y | **drā′** pə rē | *n., pl.* **drap•er•ies. 1.** Cloth hung in loose folds. **2.** Long, heavy curtains that hang in loose folds.

drows•y | **drou′** zē | *adj.* **drows•i•er, drows•i•est.** Sleepy: *I felt drowsy after the big dinner.*

drug•store | **drŭg′** stôr′ | *or* | -stōr′ | *n.* A store where prescriptions are filled.

dry | drī | *adj.* **dri•er** or **dry•er, dri•est** or **dry•est.** Not wet or damp: *A desert is dry.* —*v.* **dried, dry•ing.** To make or become dry: *She dried the dishes.*

dur•ing | **door′** ĭng | *or* | **dyoor′** - | *prep.* Throughout the course of: *Bears hibernate during the winter.*

dwin•dle | **dwĭn′** dəl | *v.* **dwin•dled, dwin•dling.** To gradually become less or smaller; shrink: *The camper's food supply began to dwindle after two weeks.*

E

ear•ly | **ûr′** lē | *adj.* **ear•li•er, ear•li•est.** In the first part; near the beginning of a time period: *the early morning.*

earn | ûrn | *v.* **1.** To get money in return for working: *to earn a living.* **2.** To win by one's efforts: *The actor earned an award.*

earth | ûrth | *n.* Often **Earth.** The third planet in the solar system. It is the planet on which human beings live.

eas•y | ē′ zē | *adj.* **eas•i•er, eas•i•est.** **1.** Not difficult: *an easy test.* **2.** Comfortable: *an easy chair.*

ech•o | ĕk′ ō | *n., pl.* **ech•oes.** A series of reflected sound waves; repeated sound. —*v.* To repeat or be repeated: *The valley echoed the gunshot.*

edge | ĕj | *n.* **1.** The place or point where something begins or ends: *the edge of the woods.* **2.** The rim or brink of something: *the edge of the cliff.*

eight | āt | *n.* A number that is one more than seven.

el•bow | ĕl′ bō | *n.* The joint between the forearm and upper arm.

em•ploy | ĕm **ploi′** | *v.* To hire and provide a livelihood for: *Mr. Jones employs 40 mechanics.*

em•ploy•er | ĕm **ploi′** ər | *n.* A person or business that employs one or more persons.

en•clo•sure | ĕn **klō′** zhər | *n.* Something that surrounds on all sides: *The pen is an enclosure for the rabbits.*

en•coun•ter | ĕn **koun′** tər | *v.* To meet, especially unexpectedly or briefly: *It was funny to encounter my teacher on a Saturday.*

en•er•gy | **ĕn′** ər jē | *n., pl.* **en•er•gies.** The ability or capability to put forth effort: *It takes energy to get the job done.*

en•joy | ĕn **joi′** | *v.* **1.** To take pleasure in: *I enjoyed that play!* **2.** To have the benefit of: *enjoys a mild climate.*

e•nough | ĭ **nŭf′** | *adj.* Sufficient to satisfy a need: *enough money for the movie.*

e•rupt | ĭ **rŭpt′** | *v.* **1.** To burst out suddenly; explode: *She was quiet, but I felt she might suddenly erupt into anger.* **2.** To become active and release lava: *No one knows when the volcano will erupt again.*

eve•ning | **ēv′** nĭng | *n.* The period of time just after sunset.

ev•er | **ĕv′** ər | *adv.* **1.** At all times; always: *He is ever ready to help.* **2.** At any time: *Did you ever hear her sing?*

eve•ry | **ĕv′** rē | *adj.* Each one of the entire number: *Every seat was filled.*

eve•ry•bod•y | **ĕv′** rē bŏd′ ē | *pron.* Every person; everyone.

eve•ry•where | **ĕv′** rē hwâr′ | *or* | -wâr′ | *adv.* In all places.

ex•ot•ic | ĭg **zŏt′** ĭk | *adj.* Foreign; unusual; strange: *I enjoyed seeing the exotic birds at the zoo.*

ex•plode | ĭk **splōd′** | *v.* **ex•plod•ed, ex•plod•ing.** **1.** To release energy with a loud noise: *The dynamite exploded.* **2.** To burst forth noisily: *The class exploded with laughter.*

ex•plore | ĭk **splôr′** | *or* | -splōr′ | *v.* **ex•plored, ex•plor•ing.** To travel through an unknown place for the purpose of discovery: *Jacques Cousteau explores the sea.*

eye•sight | **ī′** sīt′ | *n .* The ability to see; vision: *Hawks have good eyesight.*

F Fahrenheit.

fair | fâr | *adj.* **fair•er, fair•est. 1.** Just; not favoring one more than another: *a fair judge.* **2.** According to the rules: *a fair game.* **3.** Clear: *fair weather.* —*n.* A market. *These sound alike* **fare, fair.**

fam•i•ly | făm′ ə lē | *or* | făm′ lē | *n., pl.* **fam•i•lies. 1.** A parent or parents and children. **2.** All of a person's relatives.

fare | fâr | *n.* The money one pays for the cost of traveling by train, plane, bus, etc. *These sound alike* **fare, fair.**

farm•land | färm′ lănd′ | *or* | färm′ lənd | *n.* Land that is used for farming: *Corn was planted on the farmland.*

fa•tigue | fə tēg′ | *n.* The condition of being very tired or exhausted: *Mario went to bed early because of his fatigue.*

Feb•ru•ar•y | fĕb′ rōō ĕr′ ē | *or* | fĕb′ yōō- | *n.* The second month of the year. It has 28 days and in leap year 29 days.

feet | fēt |. Look up **foot.**

fence | fĕns | *n.* A railing, wall, or barrier made of boards, posts, etc. —*v.* **fenced, fenc•ing.** To enclose with a fence: *We fenced in our backyard.*

fes•tiv•i•ty | fĕ stĭv′ ĭ tē | *n., pl.* **fes•tiv•i•ties.** An activity or event that is part of observing a special occasion: *The Fourth of July festivities included a fireworks display.*

fight | fīt | *v.* **fought** | fôt |, **fight•ing. 1.** To struggle or combat with hands or weapons: *The army fought off the enemy.* **2.** To struggle in any way: *to fight for equality.* **3.** To try to overcome: *fight against cancer.*

flight | flīt | *n.* **1.** The act of flying: *a bird in flight.* **2.** An airline trip.

foe | fō | *n.* An enemy: *In the story the hero's foe tried to ruin the hero's life.*

foot | fŏŏt | *n., pl.* **feet** | fēt |. **1.** The part of the leg that touches the ground. **2.** Any base that resembles a foot: *the foot of a chair.* **3.** A unit of length equal to 12 inches.

for•ev•er | fôr ĕv′ ər | *or* | fər- | *adv.* Always; for all time.

for•get | fər gĕt′ | *v.* **for•got** | fər gŏt′ |, **for•got•ten** | fər gŏt′ n| *or* **for•got, for•get•ting.** To fail to remember: *I always seem to forget his name.*

for•got | fər gŏt′ |. Look up **forget.**

for•ti•fy | fôr′ tə fī′ | *v.* **for•ti•fied, for•ti•fy•ing, for•ti•fies. 1.** To make stronger or more secure: *The steel rods fortified the walls.* **2.** To strengthen or improve the quality of by adding something.

fox | fŏks | *n., pl.* **fox•es. 1.** A wild animal with a bushy tail and a pointed muzzle. **2.** The fur of this animal. **3.** A clever person.

freeze | frēz | *v.* **froze** | frōz |, **fro•zen** | frō′ zən |, **freez•ing. 1.** To turn from liquid to solid by removal of heat. **2.** To become covered with or turn to ice: *The pond froze.* **3.** To become motionless: *freeze with fear.*

Fri•day | frī′ dē | *or* | -dā′ | *n.* The sixth day of the week.

friend | frĕnd | *n.* A person who knows and likes another.

front | frŭnt | *n.* The forward or first part of a thing or place: *The blackboard is at the front of the room.*

froze | frōz |. Look up **freeze.**

fruit | frōōt | *n., pl.* **fruit** *or* **fruits.** The juicy, fleshy, seed-bearing part of a flowering plant.

ft foot.

fudge | fŭj | *n.* A soft candy usually made with chocolate.

full | fŏŏl | *adj.* **full•er, full•est.**
   1. Containing all that is possible; leaving no empty space: *a full tank.*
   2. Having a great many: *a room full of people.*

G

g gram.

gal. gallon.

gal•ax•y | **găl′** ək sē | *n., pl.* **gal•ax•ies.** A group of billions of stars forming a system.

geese | gēs | *n.* Look up **goose.**

germ | jûrm | *n.* A tiny organism that causes disease.

gi•ant | **jī′** ənt | *n.* Something (or someone) of great size or importance: *a sports giant.* —*adj.* Huge: *a giant watermelon.*

glad | glăd | *adj.* **glad•der, glad•dest.**
   1. Feeling pleasure or joy: *I'm glad you're here.* **2.** Willing: *glad to help.*

glove | glŭv | *n., pl.* **gloves.** A covering for the hand with separate sections for four fingers and the thumb.

go | gō | *v.* **went** | wĕnt |, **gone** | gôn | *or* | gŏn |, **go•ing.** **1.** To move along: *We're going to the store.* **2.** To depart: *You'd better go before you miss the bus.* **3.** To start: *The car won't go!*

goes | gōz |. Third person singular of **go.**

gone | gôn | *or* | gŏn |. Past participle of **go.** —*adj.* **1.** Passed: *Summer is gone now.* **2.** Absent: *My parents will be gone for two weeks.*

good-by or **good-bye** | good′ **bī′** | *interj.* Farewell: *We said "Good-by" to our cousins.*

goose | gōōs | *n., pl.* **geese** | gēs |. A water bird like a duck but larger with a longer neck.

Gov. Governor.

grass | grăs | *or* | gräs | *n.* Green, bladed plants which cover lawns, fields, and pastures.

grav•i•ty | **grăv′** ĭ tē | *n.* The force that causes objects to move toward the center of the earth.

grew | grōō |. Look up **grow.**

group | grōōp | *n.* **1.** A number of persons or things gathered together. **2.** People or things classed together for like qualities: *the vegetable group.*

grow | grō | *v.* **grew** | grōō |, **grown** | grōn |, **grow•ing.** To become large in size through a natural process: *Most plants won't grow unless they have water.*

growl | groul | *n.* A low, deep, angry sound: *the dog's growl.* —*v.* To make such a sound: *The dog growled at the mailman.*

guess | gĕs | *v.* **1.** To give an answer without really knowing. **2.** To think or believe: *I guess that's true!*

gui•tar | gĭ **tär′** | *n.* A musical instrument with strings, a fretted neck, and a pear-shaped sound box.

gym | jĭm | *n. Informal.* A gymnasium.

gym•na•si•um | jĭm **nā′** zē əm | *n.* A large room used for indoor sports.

Gyp•sy | **jĭp′** sē | *n., pl.* **Gyp•sies.** A person who belongs to a wandering group of people who came to Europe from India long ago and now live all over the world.

H

had•n't | **hăd′** nt |. Had not.

half | hăf | *or* | häf | *n., pl.* **halves** | hăvz | *or* | hävz |. One of two equal parts into which something can be divided.

hap•pen | **hăp′** ən | *v.* **1.** To come to pass: *How did this happen?* **2.** To have the fortune: *I happened to see Bill on the bus.*

have•n't | **hăv′** ənt|. Have not.

health | hĕlth | *n.* **1.** The condition of the body at any special time. **2.** A freedom from sickness or disease.

hear | hîr | *v.* **heard** | hûrd |, **hear•ing.** **1.** To take in sounds through one's ears: *Did you hear the siren?* **2.** To listen: *He loved to hear stories of the West!* **3.** To receive news: *I heard that my principal retired. These sound alike* **hear, here.**

heard | hûrd |. Look up **hear.**

heart | härt | *n.* **1.** The hollow muscular organ that pumps blood to the arteries and receives blood from the veins. **2.** The center of someone's feelings and spirit.

heav•y | **hĕv′** ē | *adj.* **heav•i•er, heav•i•est.** **1.** Having great weight: *a heavy package.* **2.** Having a large amount: *a heavy snow.*

here | hîr | *adv.* **1.** In this place: *My dad's vegetable garden is here.* **2.** At this time; now: *The singer stopped to talk to the audience here. These sound alike* **here, hear.**

high | hī | *adj.* **high•er, high•est.** **1.** Extending far up; tall: *a high building.* **2.** Above the ground: *high in the sky.* **3.** Above average: *high grades.*

high•way | **hī′** wā′ | *n.* A main public road that usually connects cities and towns.

hike | hīk | *v.* **hiked, hik•ing.** To take a long walk especially for pleasure. —*n., pl.* **hikes.** A long walk or trip on foot.

hoard | hôrd | *v.* To set aside and hide away: *Akio likes to hoard his gum instead of chewing it.*

hob•by | **hŏb′** ē | *n., pl.* **hob•bies.** A favorite pastime or activity that one likes to do: *My hobby is collecting dollhouse furniture.*

hol•low | **hŏl′** ō | *adj.* **hol•low•er, hol•low•est.** **1.** Having an opening inside; not solid; empty: *a hollow log.* —*n.* A small valley: *Sleepy Hollow.*

hope | hōp | *v.* **hoped, hop•ing.** To look forward to something with confidence that it will happen: *He hopes to become a teacher.* —*n.* A feeling of confidence: *Her words gave us hope.*

hos•pi•tal | **hŏs′** pĭ təl| *or* |-pĭt′ l | *n.* A place that provides medical and surgical care for the sick or injured.

host | hōst | *n.* A person who entertains guests: *The host of the party welcomed the guests.*

ho•tel | hō **tĕl′** | *n.* A house or large building that offers lodging and food to paying travelers, customers, etc.

hour | our | *n., pl.* **hours.** **1.** A unit of time equal to 1/12 of the time between midnight and noon; 60 minutes. **2.** A particular time of day: *My lunch hour is 1 P.M.*

hov•er | **hŭv′** ər | *v.* To stay in one place floating, flying, or fluttering in the air: *The helicopter hovered over the landing pad.*

hun•dred | **hŭn′** drĭd | *n.* A number that is equal to 10 times 10; written as 100.

hun•gry | **hŭng′** grē | *adj.* **hun•gri•er, hun•gri•est.** **1.** Desiring or needing food. **2.** Showing hunger: *The last child had a hungry look.*

hunt | hŭnt | *v.* **1.** To seek out to capture or kill for food or sport: *He hunts deer.* **2.** To search for: *The police hunted the killer.* —*n.* A hunting trip: *a fox hunt.*

hus•tle | **hŭs′** əl | *v.* **hus•tled, hus•tling.** To hurry, move, or do something quickly: *Maria hustled to finish her homework before school.*

I

I'm | īm|. I am.

im•port | ĭm pôrt′ | v. **im•port•ed, im•port•ing.** To bring in products or goods from another country for use or sale: *The grocery store was importing fruit during the winter.*

im•por•tant | ĭm pôr′ tnt | adj. **1.** Having significant value; able to determine the course of events: *an important speech.* **2.** Famous: *The President is an important person.*

in or **in.** inch.

inch | ĭnch | n., pl. **inch•es.** A unit of length equal to 1/12 of a foot.

in•side | ĭn′ sīd′ | or | ĭn sīd′ | n. The inner part or surface: *the inside of a box.*

in•ter•est•ing | ĭn′ trĭ stĭng | or | -tər ĭ stĭng | or | -tə rĕs′ tĭng | adj. Arousing interest or holding one's attention: *an interesting TV program.*

in•te•ri•or | ĭn tîr′ ē ər | n. The inner side or part; inside: *The interior of the building had five rooms.*

in•vite | ĭn vīt′ | v. **in•vit•ed, in•vit•ing.** To ask someone to come somewhere or do something: *She invited guests for dinner.*

i•ron | ī′ ərn | n. **1.** A heavy, gray metal that is easily shaped. **2.** A metal tool used to press clothes. **3.** Great strength: *a will of iron.* —v. To press: *ironing a shirt.*

is•n't | ĭz′ nt |. Is not.

itch | ĭch | n. A tickling feeling in the skin that makes one want to scratch. —v. To feel an itch: *My elbow itches.*

it'd | ĭt′ əd |. **1.** It would. **2.** It had.

J

Jan•u•ar•y | jăn′ yōō ĕr′ ē | n. The first month of the year.

jog | jŏg | v. **jogged, jog•ging. 1.** To push or nudge: *jogging someone's elbow.* **2.** To shake up: *jog my memory.* **3.** To run: *jog around the track.*

join | join | v. **1.** To connect or link: *join hands to form a circle.* **2.** To take part with others: *join a club.*

Jr. Junior.

Ju•ly | jōō lī′ | n. The seventh month of the year.

June | jōōn | n. The sixth month of the year.

jun•gle | jŭng′ gəl | n. A thick growth of tropical bushes, vines, trees, etc. extending over a large area.

Ju•pi•ter | jōō′ pĭ tər | n. The fifth planet of the solar system in order of distance from the sun. Its diameter is 86,000 miles.

K

keep | kēp | v. **kept** | kĕpt |, **keep•ing.** To hold or retain: *She keeps the key to her locker in her pocket.*

ken•nel | kĕn′ əl | n. **1.** A shelter where dogs are kept. **2.** A place where dogs are raised, trained, or cared for while their owners are away.

kg kilogram.

km kilometer.

knee | nē | n. The joint between the thigh and the lower leg.

knew | nōō | or | nyōō |. Look up **know.** *These sound alike* **knew, new.**

knife | nīf | n., pl. **knives** | nīvz |. A cutting instrument with a sharp blade and a handle.

knock | nŏk | v. **1.** To hit or strike with the fist: *knock on the head.* **2.** To make a noise by hitting on the surface: *knock on the door.* **3.** To cause to fall: *knocked off balance.*

knot | nŏt | n. A fastening made by tying cord, rope, thread, etc. —v. To tie together: *She knotted the thread.*

know | nō | v. **knew** | nōō | or | nyōō|, **known** | nōn |, **know•ing, knows. 1.** To have the facts about: *She knows her spelling words.* **2.** To be skilled in: *He knows* *how to type.* **3.** To recognize: *I know that song!*

knuck•le | **nŭk′** əl | *n.* A joint of a finger, especially one between a finger and the rest of the hand.

L

l liter.

large | lärj | *adj.* **larg•er, larg•est.** Bigger than average in size, number, etc: *A 747 is a large airplane.*

lar•va | **lär′** və | *n., pl.* **larvae** or **larvas.** The newly hatched wormlike form of some insects before they change to their adult form.

laugh | lăf | *or* | läf | *v.* To make sounds and movements to show happiness: *The audience laughed at the clown.*

lawn | lôn | *n.* A piece of ground covered with close-cut grass usually near a house.

lb. pound.

leaf | lēf | *n., pl.* **leaves** | lēvz |. **1.** A thin, flat, green part of a tree or plant that grows on the stem. **2.** A sheet of paper.

learn | lûrn | *v.* **learned** or **learnt** | lûrnt |, **learn•ing. 1.** To gain knowledge or skill: *to learn the multiplication tables.* **2.** To find out: *We learned that the game was cancelled.*

let's | lĕts |. Let us.

life | līf | *n., pl.* **lives** | līvz |. **1.** The property of living organisms that includes the ability to grow and reproduce. **2.** The period of time between birth and death. **3.** Living organisms: *plant life.*

light•ning | **līt′** nĭng | *n.* An electrical discharge in the atmosphere.

light•weight | **līt′** wāt′ | *adj.* Not weighing much; not heavy: *Lightweight clothing is cooler than a heavy sweater.*

loose | loōs | *adj.* **loos•er, loos•est. 1.** Not fastened tightly or securely: *a loose button.* **2.** Not shut in; free: *The dog was loose in our backyard.*

loud | loud | *adj.* **loud•er, loud•est.** Making or having a strong sound: *a loud song; a loud voice.*

love•ly | **lŭv′** lē | *adj.* **love•li•er, love•li•est. 1.** Having pleasing qualities; beautiful: *Those are the loveliest flowers.* **2.** Source of pleasure or fun.

loy•al | **loi′** əl | *adj.* True and faithful to a person, country, etc.

loy•al•ty | **loi′** əl tē | *n.* The condition of being faithful.

M

m. meter.

mag•ic | **măj′** ĭk | *n.* **1.** The art or pretended art of controlling forces through the use of secret charms. **2.** Special effects and tricks using sleight of hand. —*adj.* Having to do with magic: *a magic show.*

man | măn | *n., pl.* **men** | mĕn |. A full-grown male person. **man's** —*poss.* Belonging to the man.

mar•ble | **mär′** bəl | *n., pl.* **mar•bles. 1.** Crystalline rock formed by heat and pressure sometimes having colored marks: *The statue is made of marble.* **2. a.** Small, colored glass used in games. **b. marbles.** Children's game played with such balls.

March | märch | *n.* The third month of the year.

Mars | märz | *n.* The fourth planet of the solar system in order of distance from the sun.

match¹ | măch | *n.* **1.** Person or thing equal to another: *his match at tennis.* **2.** A sports contest: *a tennis match.* —*v.* **1.** To be alike: *These shoes match.* **2.** To correspond to: *He matched her running pace.*

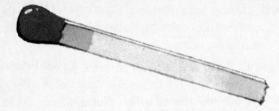

match² | măch | *n.* A strip of wood or cardboard with a substance that catches fire when rubbed on a rough surface.

may | mā | *v.* Past **might** | mīt |.
1. Possibly: *It may snow.* 2. Asking or giving permission: *May I have a cookie?*

May | mā | *n.* The fifth month of the year.

mean | mēn | *v.* **meant** | měnt |, **mean•ing, means.** 1. To have the sense of: *This means war.* 2. To be a symbol of: *Flowers mean springtime.* 3. To intend: *She meant to be helpful.*

meek | mēk | *adj.* **meek•er, meek•est.**
1. Patient; gentle. 2. Not fighting back.

men | měn | *n.* Look up **man. men's** —*poss.* Belonging to the men.

Mer•cu•ry | mûr′ kyə rē | *n.* The planet of the solar system that is closest to the sun.

me•te•or | mē′ tē ər | *or* | -ôr′ | *n.* A fragment of solid matter that enters the earth's atmosphere and burns, leaving a bright streak in the sky.

mi. mile.

mice | mīs |. Look up **mouse.**

mid•dle | mĭd′ l| *n.* 1. The point that is the same distance from each end; the center: *The turkey was in the middle of the dinner table.* 2. A point in time halfway between the beginning and the end: *The movie was funny in the middle.*

mid•night | mĭd′ nīt′ | *n.* Twelve o'clock at night. —*adj.* Of or at midnight: *a midnight ride.*

might¹ | mīt | *n.* Great power or strength: *the army's might.* **might•y** —*adj.* Strong.

might² | mīt | *v.* Past tense of **may.**

mis•sile | mĭs′ əl | *n.* An object, such as an arrow, bullet, or other weapon, that is shot through the air at a target.

mis•take | mĭ stāk′ | *n.* An act or choice that is wrong: *He made a mistake when he boarded the express bus.* —*v.* **mis•took, mis•tak•en, mis•tak•ing.** To misunderstand what one sees or hears: *I mistook that raccoon for a cat.*

mis•un•der•stand | mĭs′ ŭn dər stănd′ | *v.* **mis•un•der•stood, mis•un•der•stand•ing.** To understand incorrectly.

mis•un•der•stood | mĭs′ ŭn dər stŏŏd′ |. Look up **misunderstand.**

mod•el | mŏd′ l | *n.* 1. A small copy of something: *a model airplane.* 2. A person or thing that is a good example: *a model student.* 3. Someone who wears clothes for advertisement. —*v.* 1. To make or construct. 2. To copy. 3. To display by wearing.

mois•ture | mois′ chər | *n.* Wetness caused by water in the air, spread in small drops on a surface.

Mon•day | mŭn′ dē | *or* | -dā | *n.* The second day of the week, following Sunday and coming before Tuesday.

mon•ey | mŭn′ ē | *n., pl.* **mon•eys** or **mon•ies.** Coins of gold, silver, etc. or paper notes of fixed value issued to use in exchange for goods or services.

mon•goose | mŏng′ gōōs′ | *n.* A slender animal with a pointed face, a long tail, and the ability to catch and kill poisonous snakes. **mongoose's** —*poss.* Belonging to the mongoose: *The mongoose's quickness amazed me.*

mon•key | mŭng′ kē | *n., pl.* **mon•keys.** An animal having hands with thumbs, particularly the smaller, long-tailed animals.

month | mŭnth | *n.* One of the 12 parts into which a year is divided.

morn•ing | môr′ nĭng | *n.* The early part of the day, ending with noon..

mo•tor | mō′ tər | *n.* 1. An engine; something that produces mechanical power. 2. Something that produces motion. —*adj.* Propelled by a motor: *a motor scooter.*

mouse | mous | *n., pl.* **mice** | mīs |. A small animal with a long, narrow, hairless tail.

mouth | mouth | *n., pl.* **mouths** | mou*th*z |.
1. The opening through which animals take in food. **2.** A natural opening: *the mouth of the cave.* **3.** The opening of a container: *the mouth of a jar.*

Ms. or **Ms** | mĭs | *or* | mĭz |. An abbreviation used as a title before a woman's last name whether or not she is married.

must•'ve | **mŭst′** əv |. Must have.

N

neigh•bor | **nā′** bər | *n.* Someone who lives next door or nearby.

Nep•tune | **nĕp′** tōon′ | *or* | -tyōon′ | *n.* The eighth planet of the solar system in order of distance from the sun.

nev•er | **nĕv′** ər | *adv.* At no time; not ever: *I have never seen the Grand Canyon.*

new | nōo | *or* | nyōo | *adj.* **new•er, new•est.**
1. Recently made or formed: *a new bridge.* **2.** Just learned or discovered: *a new theory.* **3.** Never used: *a new pair of shoes.* 4. Unfamiliar: *new surroundings.* *These sound alike* **new, knew.**

news•pa•per | **nōoz′** pā′ pər | *or* | **nyōoz′**- | *n.* A daily or weekly publication printed on large sheets of paper folded together telling current news and carrying editorials, advertisements, announcements, etc.

night | nīt | *n.* **1.** The time between sunset and sunrise when it is dark. **2.** An evening devoted to a special event: *The actor was nervous on opening night.*

night•mare | **nīt′** mâr′ | *n.* **1.** A frightening dream: *Dan had a nightmare about a car crash.* **2.** A frightening experience: *The volcano was a nightmare!*

noise | noiz | *n.* **1.** A loud, harsh sound: *The noise of traffic kept me awake.* **2.** Sound of any kind: *the noise of boat whistles.*

north | nôrth | *n.* **1.** The direction 90° counterclockwise from the east; just opposite south. **2.** A region of the earth in this direction. —*adj.* Of or in the north.

nose | nōz | *n.* **1.** The part of the face that contains the nostrils and organs of smell. **2.** The sense of smell: *Mike's nose told him dinner was fried fish!* **3.** An ability to detect: *a nose for gossip.* **4.** The front end of a plane, rocket, etc.

note•book | **nōt′** bŏok′ | *n.* A book in which to write notes to be remembered or learned: *my science notebook.*

noth•ing | **nŭth′** ĭng | *pron.* Not anything: *Tim had nothing to do.* —*n.* Zero: *Any number multiplied by nothing equals nothing.*

noun | noun | *n.* A word used as the name of a person, place, thing, event, or quality.

No•vem•ber | nō **vĕm′** bər | *n.* The eleventh month of the year.

O

oak | ōk | *n.* **1.** Any of several trees with irregularly notched leaves and acorns. **2.** The hard, durable wood of this tree: *The floor is made of oak.*

o•bey | ō **bā′** | *v.* **1.** To follow or carry out a request, order, or law: *obey the stop sign.* **2.** To do what is told: *obey the teacher.*

ob•ject¹ | **ŏb′** jĭkt | *or* | -jĕkt′ | *n.*
1. Something that can be seen or touched: *a round object, a metal object.* **2.** A goal or purpose: *the object of the quiz.*

ob•ject² | əb **jĕkt′** | *v.* To oppose or protest: *The guards objected to longer working hours.*

o•cean | ō′ shən | *n.* **1.** The large mass of salt water that covers almost three-fourths of the earth's surface. **2.** The four main divisions of this mass are Atlantic, Pacific, Indian, and Arctic.

o'clock | ə klŏk′ | *adv.* Of or by the clock: *My family has dinner at six o'clock.*

Oc•to•ber | ŏk tō′ bər | *n.* The tenth month of the year.

of•fer | ô′ fər | *or* | ŏf′ ər | *v.* **1.** To present to be accepted or refused: *He offered us some candy.* **2.** To propose: *She offered some suggestions for the new playground.*

of•fer•ing | ô′ fər ĭng | *or* | ŏf′ ər ĭng | *n., pl.* **of•fer•ings.** A gift or contribution.

of•fice | ô′ fĭs | *or* | ŏf′ ĭs | *n.* **1.** A place in which business or professional work is done: *the lawyer's office.* **2.** A position: *The class held elections for the office of president.*

of•ten | ô′ fən | *or* | ŏf′ ən | *or* | ôf′ tən | *or* | ŏf′- | *adv.* Many times; frequently.

once | wŭns | *adv.* **1.** One time: *Take your vitamins once each day.* **2.** At one time in the past: *the once great ruler.*

on•ly | ōn′ lē | *adj.* One and no more; sole: *the only survivor of the plane crash.* —*adv.* Merely; just: *Only two bananas are left.*

or•bit | ôr′ bĭt | *n.* The path of a planet, satellite, or heavenly body around another body in space: *the earth's orbit around the sun.* —*v.* To put into or move about in an orbit: *The spacecraft orbits the earth.*

oth•er | ŭth′ ər | *adj.* **1.** Being the remaining one: *The other cake looks fresher.* **2.** Different: *Let's play some other game.* **3.** Extra; additional: *I have no other belt that matches this dress.* —*n.* The remaining one: *One twin likes golf; the other likes tennis.*

ours | ourz | *pron.* A possessive form of **we.** The one or ones that belong to us: *This chess set is ours.*

out•side | out sīd′ | *or* | out′ sīd′ | *n.* The outer part or surface: *the outside of the box.* —*adv.* On or to the outside: *I'm going outside with Scotty!*

o•ver•lap | ō′ vər lăp′ | *v.* **o•ver•lapped, o•ver•lap•ping.** To rest on top of or over something and cover a part of it: *A fish's scales are overlapping.*

own | ōn | *adj.* Of or belonging to oneself or itself: *my own car.* —*v.* To have or possess: *own a house.*

ox | ŏks | *n., pl.* **ox•en** | ŏk′ sən |. A full-grown male of domestic cattle that is used for farm work.

ox•en | ŏk′ sən |. Look up **ox.**

oz ounce.

P

pack•age | păk′ ĭj | *n.* A box or bundle containing one or more objects. —*v.* To place in a package.

paid | pād |. Look up **pay.**

pass | păs | *or* | päs | *v.* **1.** To go by: *We passed the carnival in the center of town.* **2.** To go through: *Oil passes through a pipe.* **3.** To be successful: *She passed the math test.* **4.** To go by in time: *He passed the hours playing his guitar.*

past | păst | *or* | päst | —*adj.* **1.** Gone by; over: *The winter is past.* **2.** Just gone by: *the past month.* —*n.* Time gone by: *We learn from the past.*

pat•i•o | păt′ ē ō′ | *n., pl.* **pat•i•os.** A paved outdoor space that is used for eating, cooking, or relaxing: *Tina's and Lisa's patios are separated by a fence.*

pause | pôz | *n.* A break in action or speech: *There was a brief pause for a commercial.* —*v.* To stop in action or speech: *The speaker paused to clear his throat.*

pay | pā | *v.* **paid** | pād |, **pay•ing.** To give money for goods or services: *We pay the baby sitter $1.00 an hour.*

peace | pēs | *n.* **1.** Freedom from war: *The war ended and there was peace throughout the land.* **2.** A calm, ordered condition: *peace and quiet.*

peach | pēch | *n., pl.* **peach•es. 1.** A sweet, round fruit with yellowish skin and a rough pit. **2.** A yellowish pink color.

pen•ny | pĕn′ ē | *n., pl.* **pen•nies.** A U.S. or Canadian coin worth one hundredth of a dollar: *100 pennies equal one dollar.*

peo•ple | pē′ pəl | *n., pl.* **peo•ple. 1.** Human beings; men, women, and children: *The bus seats 80 people.* **2.** A race; a nation: *the Norwegian people.*

pe•ri•od | pîr′ ē əd | *n.* **1.** A portion of time having a specific length or character: *a period of two months.* **2.** A punctuation mark used at the end of certain sentences.

phys•ics | fĭz′ ĭks | *n.* A science that deals with matter and energy and the laws governing them. Physics includes the study of light, motion, sound, heat, electricity, and force.

pi•an•o | pē ăn′ ō | *n., pl.* **pi•an•os.** A keyboard musical instrument in which the player sets off sound by striking the keys with the fingers.

pic•nic | pĭk′ nĭk | *n.* A pleasure trip with a meal eaten in the open air: *We went on a picnic.* —*v.* To take such a trip: *Let's picnic in the park.*

pic•ture | pĭk′ chər | *n.* **1.** A drawing, painting, photograph, etc. of some image. **2.** An image of something else: *He is the picture of health.*

pil•low | pĭl′ ō | *n.* A cloth case stuffed with feathers, down, or other soft material used to support the head while sleeping.

pitch | pĭch | *v.* **1.** To throw: *pitch a horseshoe.* **2.** In baseball, to throw a ball from the mound to the batter. **3.** To fix firmly in the ground: *pitch a tent.*

piz•za | pēt′ sə | *n.* A shallow, pie-like crust covered with cheese, tomato sauce, and spices. Italian in origin.

plain | plān | *adj.* **plain•er, plain•est.**
1. Easy to understand: *plain talk.*
2. Clear; open to view: *in plain sight.*
3. Simple: *a plain dress. These sound alike* **plain, plane.**

plane | plān | *n.* **1.** A flat or level surface. **2.** An airplane. *These sound alike* **plane, plain.**

plan•et | plăn′ ĭt | *n.* A celestial body, illuminated by light from the sun, which moves around the sun in a fixed orbit.

plas•tic | plăs′ tĭk | *n.* Any of a group of substances made chemically and molded by heat to form sheets, fibers, bottles, etc.

please | plēz | *v.* **pleased, pleas•ing. 1.** To give pleasure to: *The gift pleased Mom.* **2.** Wish: *Do as you please.*

plen•ty | plĕn′ tē | *n.* A full supply; all that is needed: *plenty of food.*

Plu•to | plōō′ tō | *n.* The ninth planet of the solar system in order of distance from the sun.

pock•et | pŏk′ ĭt | *n., pl.* **pock•ets.** A small pouch sewn into clothing and used to hold things.

po•em | pō′ əm | *n.* A composition, usually in verse, with language meant to vividly express an image or experience.

point | point | *n.* **1.** The sharp end of something: *the point of the pencil.* **2.** A place or position: *the starting point.* **3.** A degree: *the freezing point.*

point•less | **point′** lĭs | *adj.* Senseless; meaningless: *Juan thought the argument was pointless.*

poise | poiz | *n.* The ability to appear calm and confident: *Poise will help you impress others.* —*v.* **poised, pois•ing.** To balance or be balanced: *The cat poised for the jump onto the table.*

poi•son | **poi′** zən | *n.* Any substance dangerous to life and health: *Bottles containing poison are clearly marked.* —*v.* To kill or harm with poison.

po•lice | pə **lēs′** | *n., pl.* **po•lice. 1.** The part of the government that maintains order and enforces the law. **2.** The members of this department.

po•ny | **pō′** nē | *n., pl.* **po•nies.** Any of several kinds of small horses.

pop•corn | **pŏp′** kôrn′ | *n.* A kind of corn with kernels that burst open and puff out when heated.

pow•er•ful | **pou′** ər fəl | *adj.* Having great power or force: *a powerful engine; a powerful country.*

pre•cau•tion | prĭ **kô′** shən | *n.* Something that is done beforehand to guard against harm, danger, mistakes, or accidents.

Pres. President.

prob•lem | **prŏb′** ləm | *n.* A question that presents confusion or difficulty: *Keeping peace is a universal problem.*

pro•gram | **prō′** grăm | *or* | -grəm | *n.* **1.** An ordered list of events for a performance, presentation, etc. **2.** The performance or presentation; a show.

proud | proud | *adj.* **proud•er, proud•est. 1.** Feeling of pleasure over something one owns, is, or does: *proud to be a farmer.* **2.** Having self-respect: *too proud to ask.*

pt. pint.

pud•ding | **pŏod′** ĭng | *n.* A sweet custard-like dessert: *chocolate pudding.*

pull | pŏol | *v.* **1.** To move toward oneself through grasping and drawing with force: *pulling the cart.* **2.** To put on: *pull on the mittens.*

pur•ple | **pûr′** pəl | *n.* A color produced by mixing red and blue pigments. —*adj.* Of the color: *a purple dress.*

Q

q. quart.

quart | kwôrt | *n.* A unit of volume used for measuring liquid, equal to two pints.

queen | kwēn | *n.* **1.** A female monarch: *Queen Elizabeth.* **2.** A woman who is very important: *the queen of jazz.*

quick | kwĭk | *adj.* **quick•er, quick•est. 1.** Moving with speed; fast: *The cowboy was quick on the draw.* **2.** Done in a short time: *a quick lunch.* **3.** Bright; alert: *a quick wit.*

qui•et | **kwī′** ĭt | *adj.* **qui•et•er, qui•et•est. 1.** Making little or no sound: *the quiet baby.* **2.** Not moving; still: *The steamboat floated down the quiet river.*

qui•et•ness | **kwī′** ĭt nəs | *n.* Silence: *The quietness in the classroom was unusual.*

R

ra•di•o | **rā′** dē ō | *n., pl.* **ra•di•os. 1.** The use of electromagnetic waves to carry messages without the use of wires. **2.** The equipment used to carry such sound. —*v.* To send messages in this manner.

rail•road | **rāl′** rōd′ | *n.* A road or track built with parallel steel rails and used by trains.

Rd. Road.

read•y | **rĕd′** ē | *adj.* **read•i•er, read•i•est. 1.** Prepared for action or use: *getting* *ready for the trip.* **2.** Willing: *ready to accept the offer.*

rea•son | **rē′** zən | *n.* A cause for acting, thinking, or feeling a special way. —*v.* **1.** To conclude. **2.** To argue.

re•gard•less | rĭ **gärd′** lĭs | *adv.* Without concern for problems or objections; anyway: *The children play outside regardless of the weather.*

reign | rān | *n.* The time that a king or queen rules. —*v.* To rule as a king or queen. *These sound alike* **reign, rain, rein.**

re•ply | rĭ **plī′** | *v.* **re•plied, re•ply•ing, re•plies.** To give an answer: *He replied with anger.* —*n.* An answer: *His reply was incorrect.*

re•port | rĭ **pôrt′** | *or* | **-pōrt′** | *n.* An oral or written account containing information in an organized form: *His report was about the capital of Brazil.* —*v.* To give an account of something: *to report the baseball scores.*

re•trieve | rĭ **trēv′** | *v.* **re•trieved, re•triev•ing.** To get back: *We will retrieve the baseballs we hit.*

re•vive | rĭ **vīv′** | *v.* **re•vived, re•viv•ing. 1.** To come or bring back to life or consciousness. **2.** To give new strength to.

re•volve | rĭ **vŏlv′** | *v.* **re•volved, re•volv•ing.** To move in a circle or orbit: *Planets revolve around the sun.*

RFD *or* **R.F.D.** Rural Free Delivery.

right | rīt | *n.* **1.** The side opposite the left: *The driver signaled to the right.* **2.** That which is fitting or good: *right or wrong.* —*adj.* Of or located to the opposite of the left: *the right foot.*

rock¹ | rŏk | *n., pl.* **rocks. 1.** Any hard, natural material of mineral origin; stone. **2.** The mineral matter that makes up a large portion of the earth's crust.

rock² | rŏk | *v.* To move backward and forward, or from side to side: *The waves rocked the boat!*

root | rōot | *n.* The part of the plant that grows into the soil and absorbs water

and minerals. *These sound alike* **root, route.**

ro•tate | **rō′** tāt′ | *v.* **ro•tat•ed, ro•tat•ing. 1.** To turn around a center or axis. **2.** To change in a regular order: *The team rotated around the volleyball court.*

rough | rŭf | *adj.* **rough•er, rough•est. 1.** Not smooth or even: *a rough trail.* **2.** Coarse to the touch: *rough sandpaper.* **3.** Not gentle: *a rough, tough bully.*

route | rōot | *or* | rout | *n.* A road for traveling from one place to another: *We took the coastal route to Los Angeles. These sound alike* **route, root.**

roy•al | **roi′** əl | *adj.* **1.** Of kings and queens: *the royal palace.* **2.** Fit for a king or queen: *royal treatment.*

Rte. Route.

ru•ral | **rŏor′** əl | *adj.* Having to do with, in, or like the country, country people, or life in the country: *My family bought a house in a rural area.*

S

sat•el•lite | **săt′** l īt′ | *n.* **1.** A celestial body that revolves around a planet: *The moon is a satellite of the earth.* **2.** An artificial object launched to orbit the earth or other celestial bodies.

Sat•ur•day | **săt′** ər dē | *or* | **-dā′** | *n.* The seventh day of the week.

Sat•urn | **săt′** ərn | *n.* The sixth planet of the solar system in order of distance from the sun.

save | sāv | *v.* **saved, sav•ing. 1.** To rescue from harm or danger. **2.** To keep for future use; to store: *save the leftovers.*

scarf | skärf | *n., pl.* **scarfs** *or* **scarves** | skärvz |. A triangular or rectangular piece of cloth worn around the head, neck, or shoulders.

score | skôr | *or* | skōr | *n.* The total number of points made by a player or team in a game or contest. —*v.* To make points in a game or contest: *He scored 12 points.*

scream | skrēm | *v.* To make a loud, sharp cry: *She screamed during the horror movie.* —*n.* A loud cry.

sea•son | sē′ zən | *n.* **1.** One of four divisions of the year: spring, summer, autumn, and winter. **2.** A time of the year devoted to a certain activity: *baseball season.*

se•cret | sē′ krĭt | *adj.* **1.** Kept from general knowledge: *secret missions.* **2.** Set apart: *a secret hideaway. —n.* Something known only to oneself or a few: *Can you keep a secret?*

seem | sēm | *v.* To appear to be: *He seems angry about the judge's decision.*

Sep•tem•ber | sĕp tĕm′ bər | *n.* The ninth month of the year.

shad•ow | shăd′ ō | *n.* The outline cast by an object blocking the light's rays.

shape | shāp | *n.* **1.** An outline or form: *the shape of a circle.* **2.** A form or condition in which something exists: *The old barn was in good shape. —v.* To mold or give a form to: *shape the clay.*

share | shâr | *v.* **shared, shar•ing. 1.** To use, experience, or enjoy with others: *share the pie.* **2.** To disclose to others: *share the information with the police. —n.* A portion: *a share of the estate.*

sharp | shärp | *adj.* **sharp•er, sharp•est. 1.** Having a thin cutting edge: *a sharp knife.* **2.** Abrupt: *a sharp drop in the mountain.* **3.** Clear: *a sharp picture.* **4.** Quick and forceful: *a sharp slap.* **5.** Having a strong odor or flavor: *a sharp taste.*

she'd | shēd |. **1.** She had. **2.** She would.

sheep | shēp | *n., pl.* **sheep.** An animal with a fleecy coat which is used for wool.

shelf | shĕlf | *n., pl.* **shelves** | shĕlvz |. A flat, rectangular piece of metal, wood, etc. fastened to a wall and used to store things.

shelves | shĕlvz |. Look up **shelf.**

sher•iff | shĕr′ ĭf | *n.* The county officer in charge of making sure the law is obeyed.

shoot | sho͞ot | *v.* **shot** | shŏt |, **shoot•ing. 1.** To hit, wound, or kill with a bullet, arrow, etc.: *The hunter shot the rabbit.* **2.** To aim for: *shooting for a record-breaking marathon run.*

shore | shôr | *or* | shōr | *n.* The land along the edge of a sea, lake, etc.

should | shoŏd |. Past tense of **shall.** Ought to: *You should study for the test.*

should•n't | shoŏd′ nt |. Should not.

should•'ve | shoŏd′ əv |. Should have.

show•er | shou′ ər | *n.* **1.** A short fall of rain. **2.** A steady flow of something: *a shower of gifts.* **3.** A shower bath. **4.** A party to honor someone: *a baby shower. —v.* **1.** To pour down in a shower. **2.** To bestow: *The grandparents showered the baby with love.*

sight | sīt | *n.* **1.** The ability to see: *My sight is better with glasses.* **2.** Thing seen; something worth seeing: *the sight of Paris. —v.* To see or observe.

sim•ple | sĭm′ pəl | *adj.* **sim•pler, sim•plest. 1.** Easy; not complicated: *a simple game.* **2.** Not showy: *a simple suit; simple food.*

size | sīz | *n.* **1.** The amount of space that something takes up: *These two boxes are the same size.* **2.** The extent or amount: *the size of the factory.*

ski | skē | *n., pl.* **skis** or **ski.** One of a pair of long, flat, wood or metal runners used for gliding on snow or water. *—v.* **skied, ski•ing.** To glide or move on skis.

ski•er | skē′ ər | *n.* A person who skis: *The beginning skier went down the low hill.*

skirt | skûrt | *n.* **1.** The part of the dress that hangs from the waist. **2.** A separate piece of clothing that hangs from the waist.

slide | slīd | *v.* **slid** | slĭd |, **slid•ing. 1.** To move smoothly along a surface: *to slide the drawers back and forth.* **2.** To slip: *slide on ice. —n.* A sliding action or movement: *a rock slide.*

slow | slō | *adj.* **slow•er, slow•est. 1.** Not moving quickly: *The mule is a slow animal.* **2.** Requiring a long time: *slow to show his anger.* **—slow′ly** *adv.*

smart | smärt | *adj.* **smart•er, smart•est.**
1. Bright; intelligent: *a smart child.*
2. Fashionable: *a smart new dress.* —*v.*
To feel a stinging pain: *That bee sting really smarts!*

smile | smīl | *n.* An expression formed by the upward curve of the mouth to show pleasure, amusement, etc. —*v.* To look pleased or amused: *He smiled as he watched the playful dog.*

snack | snăk | *n.* **1.** A light meal. **2.** Food eaten between a regular meal.

soap | sōp | *n.* A cleansing agent, usually made of fat and lye, manufactured as bars, flakes, liquid, etc.

soil[1] | soil | *n.* The top layer of the earth's surface in which seeds are planted.

soil[2] | soil | *v.* To make or become dirty: *He soiled his white T-shirt.*

solar system | sō′ lər sĭs′ təm | *n.* The sun and all the planets, satellites, etc. that revolve around it.

solve | sŏlv | *v.* **solved, solv•ing.** To find the answer to: *She solved the problem by herself.*

some•how | sŭm′ hou′ | *adv.* In some way: *I knew that I'd get there somehow.*

some•time | sŭm′ tīm′ | *adv.* At one time or another: *It happened sometime last winter.*

sor•ry | sŏr′ ē | *or* | sôr′ ē | *adj.* **sor•ri•er, sor•ri•est.** Feeling pity or regret: *I'm sorry that you don't feel well.*

soup | sōōp | *n.* A liquid food made by boiling meat, vegetables, etc.

sour | sour | *adj.* **1.** Having a sharp, biting taste; acid: *Lemonade is sour.*
2. Spoiled: *sour milk.* **3.** Bad-tempered: *a sour face.*

south | south | *n.* **1.** The direction 90° clockwise from the direction of the sunrise; just opposite north. **2.** The region of the earth that lies in this direction. —*adj.* Of or in the south.

sow | sō | *v.* **sowed, sown** or **sowed, sow•ing.** To scatter seeds over the ground to produce a crop: *Amy is going to sow the carrot seeds in her garden. These sound alike* **sow, sew, so.**

soy•bean | soi′ bēn′ | *n.* Also **soya bean.** A bean plant grown for its edible, nutritious seeds.

space | spās | *n.* **1.** The unlimited area in which the solar system, stars, and galaxies exist. **2.** Any blank or empty area: *The space beside the tree will be used for my garden.*

speak | spēk | *v.* **spoke** | spōk |, **spok•en** | spō′ kən |, **speak•ing. 1.** To utter words: *She spoke excitedly about horseback riding.* **2.** To give a speech: *The mayor will speak on TV.* **3.** To use a language: *I speak Spanish and French.*

spe•cial | spĕsh′ əl | *adj.* **1.** Not common or usual; exceptional: *a special event.*
2. Distinct from others: *a special lock that sets off an alarm.* **3.** Having a particular function or purpose: *special skills.*

speech | spēch | *n.* **1.** The act of speaking. **2.** The ability to speak. **3.** A talk or address: *the governor's speech.*

spoil | spoil | *v.* **spoiled** or **spoilt** | spoilt |, **spoil•ing. 1.** To damage or injure so as to make useless: *The bad weather spoiled the garden party.* **2.** To become rotten or decayed: *spoiled milk.* **3.** To indulge too much: *spoil the child.*

sponge | spŭnj | *n.* **1.** A simple water animal having a soft, elastic skeleton with many pores. **2.** The absorbent skeleton of any of these animals used for soaking, cleaning, etc.

spy | spī | *n., pl.* **spies. 1.** An agent paid to secretly obtain information. **2.** Person who secretly watches another. —*v.* To keep secret watch.

squad | skwŏd | *n.* **1.** A small group of soldiers who work, train, and fight together. **2.** A small group of people who work together toward a goal. **3.** A sports team.

square | skwâr | *n.* **1.** A rectangle with four equal sides. **2.** Any figure with this shape. **3.** An open area at the intersection of two streets.

squeeze | skwēz | *v.* **squeezed, squeez•ing.** **1.** To press hard upon: *squeeze the stuffed animal.* **2.** To put pressure on to extract liquid: *squeeze a lemon.* **3.** To force one's way: *squeeze through the door.* **4.** To crowd: *squeeze into the bus.*

squirt | skwûrt | *v.* **1.** To force out through a narrow opening. **2.** To come out in a jet or stream.

St. Street.

stair | stâr | *n.* **stairs.** A series or flight of steps.

stamp | stămp | *v.* **1.** To set the foot down heavily: *Stamp your wet shoes on the floor.* **2.** To strike with an object that leaves a mark or message. **3.** To put postage on. —*n.* **1.** An object that leaves a mark when pressed on something. **2.** A piece of gummed paper with a special mark: *a postage stamp.*

stand | stănd | *v.* **stood** | stŏŏd |, **stand•ing.** To stay in an upright position on the feet.

stare | stâr | *v.* **stared, star•ing, stares.** To look at with a steady gaze: *He stared at the famous movie star.*

state | stāt | *n.* **1.** A condition: *the state of my bank account.* **2.** A mood: *an angry state.* **3.** A group of people living under an independent government: *the state of Israel.* **4.** One of 50 subdivisions of the U.S.: *the state of Virginia.*

steal | stēl | *v.* **stole** | stōl |, **stol•en** | stō′ lən |, **steal•ing.** **1.** To take without permission. **2.** To move or pass without making noise: *steal through the bushes.*

stole | stōl |. Look up **steal.**

stom•ach | stŭm′ ək | *n.* A large, muscular bag in the body that receives food,

digests some of it, and passes it on to the intestines.

stood | stŏŏd |. Look up **stand.**

sto•ry | stôr′ ē | *or* | stōr′ ē | *n., pl.* **sto•ries.** An account of something either true or fictitious: *a story about a mountain adventure.*

stow | stō | *v.* To put away or store for future use; pack: *We stow our bicycles in the garage.*

straw | strô | *n.* Stalks of grain after drying and threshing used as stuffing or padding, or for weaving hats, baskets, etc.

stretch | strĕch | *v.* **1.** To draw out or pull: *Elastic stretches.* **2.** To extend across a given space: *This route stretches across two states.* **3.** To extend one's body or limbs: *stretch out on the couch.*

strong | strông | *or* | strŏng | *adj.* **strong•er, strong•est.** **1.** Physically powerful: *a strong person.* **2.** Able to take stress or strain: *a strong chair.* **3.** Intense in degree: *strong feelings.*

stud•y | stŭd′ ē | *n., pl.* **stud•ies.** The effort to learn by reading and thinking: *hours of study.* —*v.* **stud•ied, stud•y•ing.** To apply one's mind to gaining knowledge: *to study science.*

sub•ject | sŭb′ jĭkt | *adj.* Under the power of another: *subject to the will of the king.* —*n.* **1.** A person or thing that something is about: *the subject of the book.* **2.** An area of study: *Music is my favorite subject.*

sud•den | sŭd′ n | *adj.* Happening at once without warning: *a sudden crack of thunder.* —**sud•den•ly** *adv.*

sug•ar | shŏŏg′ ər | *n.* A sweet substance made from sugar cane or sugar beets and used in food products.

sum•mer | sŭm′ ər | *n.* The season of the year between spring and autumn.

Sun•day | sŭn′ dē | *or* | -dā′ | *n.* The first day of the week.

sun•shine | sŭn′ shīn′ | *n.* **1.** The light of the sun. **2.** Happiness.

sup•ply | sə plī′ | *v.* **sup•plied, sup•ply•ing, sup•plies.** To provide: *Trees supply paper goods and wood products.* —*n.* The amount available: *Our pencil supply is low.*

sur•prise | sər prīz′ | *v.* **sur•prised, sur•pris•ing. 1.** To come upon suddenly: *I was surprised by the raccoon in the attic.* **2.** To cause to feel astonished: *Her early arrival surprised me.* —*n.* Something sudden and unexpected: *The party came as a surprise!*

swal•low¹ | swŏl′ ō | *v.* To take into the stomach through the throat: *swallow food.*

swal•low² | swŏl′ lō | *n.* A swift-flying bird with long, pointed wings.

sweat•er | swĕt′ ər | *n.* A knitted garment worn on the upper part of the body.

sweep | swēp | *v.* **swept** | swĕpt |, **sweep•ing.** To clean or clear with a broom or brush: *Sweep the floor!*

sweet | swēt | *adj.* **sweet•er, sweet•est. 1.** Having a taste like that of sugar or honey. **2.** Having a pleasant smell: *the sweet smell of flowers.* **3.** Lovable.

swim | swĭm | *v.* **swam** | swăm |, **swum** | swŭm |, **swim•ming.** To move through the water through movements of the body or parts of the body.

swoosh | swo͝osh | *or* | swo͞osh | *v.* To make a rushing sound: *The water swooshed down the drain.*

take•off | tāk′ ôf′ | *n.* The act of leaving the ground in flight: *The takeoff of the airplane was on time.*

taste | tāst | *n.* **1.** The sense that distinguishes flavor qualities of things placed in the mouth. **2.** The flavor itself: *a sour taste.* —*v.* **tast•ed, tast•ing.** To distinguish the flavor by taking in the mouth.

taught | tôt |. Look up **teach.**

teach | tēch | *v.* **taught** | tôt |, **teach•ing. 1.** To give instruction: *She teaches math.* **2.** To show how to do: *Bobby taught me how to swim.*

tech•nol•o•gy | tĕk nŏl′ ə jē | *n., pl.* **tech•nol•o•gies. 1.** The use of science for practical purposes: *Technology is used in developing computers.* **2.** The methods, machines, and materials used in a science or type of work.

teeth | tēth |. Look up **tooth.**

that | thăt | *or* | thət *when unstressed* | *adj., pl.* **those** | thōz |. Being the one singled out: *that child; that building.*

that's | thăts |. That is.

their | thâr | *or* | thər *when unstressed* | *pron.* Belonging to them: *their dog. These sound alike* **their, there, they're.**

there | thâr | *adv.* In or at that place: *The book is over there. These sound alike* **there, their, they're.**

there•'re | thâr′ ər |. There are.

they'll | thāl |. They will.

they're | thâr |. They are.

they've | thāv |. They have.

thick | thĭk | *adj.* **thick•er, thick•est. 1.** With much space in depth or from side to side: *a thick wall.* **2.** Measuring between two sides: *three feet thick.* **3.** Heavy: *a thick coat of fur.*

thief | thēf | *n., pl.* **thieves.** A person who steals.

third | thûrd | *adj.* Next after second: *the third man at bat.*

those | *thōz* | *pron.* Plural of **that.** Used to point out several persons or things: *those children; those houses.*

though | *thō* | *adv.* However; nevertheless: *That doll is pretty; the price is too high, though.*

thought | thôt | *n.* **1.** The process of thinking. **2.** An idea: *She had some thoughts about decorating the room.* —*v.* Past tense of think: *I thought that the movie was great.*

throat | thrōt | *n.* The part of the digestive system between the back of the mouth and the esophagus.

through | thro͞o | *prep.* **1.** In one side and out the opposite side of: *through the tunnel.* **2.** Among; in the midst of: *through the woods. These sound alike* **through, threw.**

Thurs•day | **thûrz′** dē | *or* | -dā′ | *n.* The fifth day of the week.

tick•le | **tĭk′** əl | *v.* **tick•led, tick•ling.** **1.** To feel a tingling sensation. **2.** To touch lightly. **3.** To amuse.

tie | tī | *v.* **tied, ty•ing.** **1.** To fasten with a string or cord: *tie a package.* **2.** To make a bow or knot. **3.** To equal in a contest: *tie the score.* —*n.* **1.** A cord that ties something. **2.** A necktie. **3.** A bond. **4.** Equality in scores.

toe | tō | *n.* One of the five digits at the end of a foot.

to•geth•er | tə **gĕth′** ər | *or* | to͞o- | *adv.* **1.** With each other: *Our family was together for Thanksgiving.* **2.** At the same time: *We applauded together.*

toil | toil | *v.* To work hard for a long time: *Matt toiled in the garden pulling weeds.* —*n.* Hard work.

to•mor•row | tə **mŏr′** ō | *or* | -**môr′** ō | *n.* The day after today.

to•night, also **to-night** | tə **nīt′** | *adv.* On or during this night: *It may rain tonight.* —*n.* The night of this day: *Tonight is New Year's Eve.*

too | to͞o | *adv.* **1.** Also: *Jim is coming too.* **2.** More than enough: *That bundle is too heavy. These sound alike* **too, to, two.**

tooth | to͞oth | *n., pl.* **teeth** | tēth |. Any of the hard, bony structures found in the mouth and set in sockets around the jaw.

tor•ture | **tôr′** chər | *v.* To cause great pain to someone or something: *Don't torture yourself by worrying too much.* —*n.* **1.** The act of causing severe pain or suffering. **2.** Great pain or suffering: *Speaking in front of the class is torture for some students.*

to•tal | **tōt′** l | *n.* **1.** The sum of numbers in addition. **2.** Whole: *The total cost of the car is $5,000.*

touch | tŭch | *v.* **1.** To come into contact with: *The curtains touch the floor.* **2.** To feel with the hands: *Please don't touch the glass!*

tough | tŭf | *adj.* **tough•er, tough•est.** **1.** Strong: *Mules are tough animals.* **2.** Hard to chew: *a tough piece of meat.* **3.** Not easy: *a tough exam.*

to•ward | tôrd | *or* | tōrd | *or* | tə **wôrd′** | *prep.* **1.** In the direction of: *toward the lake.* **2.** Shortly before; near: *toward evening.*

tow•el | **tou′** əl | *n.* A piece of cloth or paper used for wiping or drying.

tow•er | **tou′** ər | *n.* A high structure standing alone or forming part of a church, castle, or other building.

trade | trād | *n.* The business of buying and selling: *trade between countries.* —*v.* **trad•ed, trad•ing.** **1.** To engage in buying and selling: *trading with the settlers.* **2.** To exchange: *He traded two baseball cards for the marbles.*

trag•ic | **trăj′** ĭk | *adj.* Very sad, unfortunate, or dreadful: *We heard about the tragic accident on the news.*

trail | trāl | *v.* **1.** To drag along the ground. **2.** To track: *The police dogs trailed the convict.* —*n.* A path across an unsettled region.

trav•el | **trăv′** əl | *v.* **trav•eled** or **trav•elled, trav•el•ing** or **trav•el•ling. 1.** To go from one place to another: *travel around the city by bus.* **2.** To be transmitted: *Sound travels through the air.*

tread | trĕd | *v.* **trod, trod•den,** or **trod. 1.** To walk on, over, or along: *Matt trod through the tall grass.* **2.** To trample.

trea•son | **trē′** zən | *n.* The crime of helping the enemy of a group or country one is loyal to: *Giving plans of attack to the enemy is treason.*

treat | trēt | *v.* **1.** To act toward: *The judge treated him fairly.* **2.** To provide food or entertainment for: *We were treated to a movie.* —*n.* **1.** A source of delight: *The circus was a treat.* **2.** The act of treating.

tree | trē | *n., pl.* **trees.** A tall, woody plant with branches and a main stem or trunk.

trou•ble | **trŭb′** əl | *n.* **1.** Difficulty: *having trouble unlocking the suitcase.* **2.** A difficult situation: *The lost child was in trouble.* **3.** Extra work or effort: *Don't go to any trouble!*

tru•ly | **trōō′** lē | *adv.* Sincerely: *I'm truly happy that you're here.*

truth | trōōth | *n., pl.* **truths** | trōōthz | *or* | trōōths |. The real state of a thing; that which is the case: *Tell the truth.*

try | trī | *v.* **tried, try•ing, tries. 1.** To sample in order to determine quality: *try the new vacuum cleaner.* **2.** To hear in a court of law. **3.** To attempt: *try to run in the marathon.*

Tues•day | **tōōz′** dē | *or* | -dā′ | *or* | **tyōōz′**- | *n.* The third day of the week.

twice | twīs | *adv.* Two times: *He has visited San Francisco twice.*

two | tōō | *n.* The number that follows one. *These sound alike* **two, too, to.**

U

un•der | **ŭn′** dər | *prep.* **1.** Below: *under the bed.* **2.** Beneath the surface: *under the sea.* **3.** Less than: *under $5.00.*

un•der•stand | ŭn′ dər **stănd′** | *v.* **un•der•stood** | ŭn′ dər **stŏŏd′** |, **un•der•stand•ing. 1.** To grasp the nature of: *understand science.* **2.** To know thoroughly: *He understands Spanish.* **3.** To realize: *I understand how hard you work!*

un•dis•cov•ered | ŭn dĭ **skŭv′** ərd | *adj.* Not found: *Scientists search for undiscovered cures for diseases.*

United States of America | yōō **nīt′** ĭd stāts ûv ə **měr′** ĭ kə | *n.* A country in North America consisting of 50 states and the District of Columbia.

u•ni•verse | **yōō′** nə vûrs′ | *n.* The whole of existing things; the cosmos.

un•til | ŭn **tĭl′** | *prep.* **1.** Up to the time of: *The awards dinner lasted until 10 o'clock.* **2.** Before: *She won't leave until morning.*

un•time•ly | ŭn **tīm′** lē | *adj.* **un•time•li•er, un•time•li•est. 1.** Happening at the wrong or improper time: *The girl's untimely sneeze in the play embarrassed her.* **2.** Happening too soon: *The untimely blooming of the flowers was due to the mild winter.*

up•stairs | **ŭp′** stârz′ | *adv.* Up the stairs. —*n.* The upper floor.

U•ra•nus | **yōōr′** ə nəs | *or* | yōō **rā′**- | *n.* The seventh planet of the solar system in increasing distance from the sun.

u•ten•sil | yōō **těn′** səl | *n.* A tool or object that is useful for making or doing something: *Knives and forks are utensils used for eating.*

V

var•nish | **vär′** nĭsh | *n., pl.* **var•nish•es.** A liquid-like paint that gives a thin, hard, clear surface. —*v.* To cover with varnish.

vast•ness | **văst′** nəs | *n.* Greatness in area or size; hugeness: *The vastness of the ocean is amazing.*

Ve•nus | **vē′** nəs | *n.* The second planet of the solar system in increasing distance from the sun.

vil•lage | **vĭl′** ĭj | *n.* A group of houses that form a community, usually smaller than a town.

voice | vois | *n.* Sounds made by the respiratory system that come through the mouth: *Her voice was loud and raspy.*

vol•can•ic | vŏl **kăn′** ĭk | *adj.* Of or produced by a volcano: *When the volcano exploded, there was volcanic ash everywhere.*

vow•el | **vou′** əl | *n.* **1.** A voiced speech sound produced by not blocking the breath. **2.** A letter that represents such a sound, as *a, e, i, o,* or *u.*

voy•age | **voi′** ĭj | *n* . A long journey made by a ship or sometimes by an aircraft or spacecraft. —*v.* To travel in this way.

W

waist | wāst | *n.* The part of the human body between the ribs and the hips. *These sound alike* **waist, waste.**

wait | wāt | *v.* To stay or stop doing something until someone or something comes: *Wait until the plane lands. These sound alike* **wait, weight.**

wal•let | **wŏl′** ĭt | *n.* A small, flat, leather case for holding paper money, coins, photographs, etc.

wan•der | **wŏn′** dər | *v.* To travel from place to place freely; roam: *wander around the shopping mall.*

warm | wôrm | *adj.* **warm•er, warm•est.** Moderately hot; having some heat: *warm water; warm weather.*

wash | wŏsh | *or* | wôsh | *v.* **1.** To clean with water and often soap: *wash your hands.* **2.** To be removed or carried by moving water: *High tide washed away the seashells.* —*n.* A batch of clothes that are to be or have just been washed.

was•n't | **wŏz′** ənt | *or* | **wŭz′** -|. Was not.

waste | wāst | *v.* **wast•ed, wast•ing.** To spend or use up foolishly: *He wasted his money on that awful movie! These sound alike* **waste, waist.**

watch | wŏch | *v.* **1.** To look at: *Watch the birds in flight!* **2.** To be on the lookout: *Watch out for falling rocks!* —*n.* A small timepiece worn on the wrist or on a chain.

wa•ter | **wô′** tər | *or* | **wŏt′** ər | *n.* A liquid made up of hydrogen and oxygen that covers three fourths of the earth's surface. —*v.* To sprinkle or moisten with water.

weath•er | **wĕ***th***′** ər | *n.* The condition of the atmosphere with regard to temperature, moisture, wind, etc.

Wednes•day | **wĕnz′** dē | *or* | -dā′ | *n.* The fourth day of the week.

week•end | **wēk′** ĕnd′ | *n.* The end of the week, especially the time from Friday evening to Sunday evening.

weight | wāt | *n.* **1.** The force with which a body is attracted to the earth or other celestial bodies: *Our weight is less on the moon.* **2.** How heavy a thing is: *The baby's weight is 16 pounds. These sound alike* **weight, wait.**

we're | wîr |. We are.

weren't | wûrnt | *or* | **wûr′** ənt|. Were not.

where | hwâr | *or* | wâr | *adv.* At or in what place: *Where is the dog?*

wheth•er | **hwĕ***th***′** ər | *or* | **wĕ***th***′** - | *conj.*
1. Used to express choice: *whether to walk or drive.* **2.** If: *I asked whether I should wash the chalkboard.*

whis•tle | **hwĭs′** əl | *or* | **wĭs′-** | *v.* **whis•tled, whis•tling.** To make a clear, high-pitched sound by forcing breath through the teeth or by pursing the lips. —*n.* Instrument used for whistling.

wife | wīf | *n., pl.* **wives** | wīvz |. A woman to whom a man is married. **wife's** —*poss.* Belonging to a wife.

will | wĭl | *v.* Past **would** | wŏŏd |. Used to indicate future action or condition: *They will go bowling tonight.*

win | wĭn | *v.* **won** | wŭn |, **win•ning. 1.** To achieve victory over others: *win a game.* **2.** To receive an award for performance: *He won the Nobel Prize for his research in science.*

win•dow | **wĭn′** dō | *n.* **1.** An opening in a wall to let in light or air. **2.** A pane of glass.

win•ter | **wĭn′** tər | *n.* The season of the year between autumn and spring.

wise | wīz | *adj.* **wis•er, wis•est. 1.** Having wisdom or good judgment. **2.** Showing common sense.

with•out | wĭ*th* **out′** | *or* | wĭ*th*- | *prep.* Not having; lacking: *without money; without food.*

wolf | wŏŏlf | *n., pl.* **wolves** | wŏŏlvz |. A flesh-eating animal related to the dog.

wom•an | **wŏŏm′** ən | *n., pl.* **wom•en** | **wĭm′** ĭn |. A full-grown female human being. **woman's** —*poss.* Belonging to the woman. **women's** —*poss.* Belonging to the women.

won | wŭn |. Look up **win.**

won•der•ful | **wŭn′** dər fəl | *adj.* Marvelous; remarkable: *a wonderful trip.*

won•drous | **wŭn′** drəs | *adj.* Remarkable; marvelous: *Two rainbows in the sky at the same time is a wondrous sight.*

wood•en | **wŏŏd′** n | *adj.* Made of wood: *a wooden table.*

wool | wŏŏl | *n.* The soft, curly hair of sheep used for yarn and clothing.

world | wûrld | *n.* **1.** The earth. **2.** All of certain parts, people, or things of the world: *the sports world; the animal world.*

worth•while | **wûrth′** wīl′ | *adj.* Important enough to be worth the time, effort, or money spent: *Reading a good book is worthwhile.*

would | wŏŏd |. Look up **will.**

would•n't | **wŏŏd′** nt |. Would not.

wrin•kle | **rĭng′** kəl | *n.* A small ridge or crease on a normally smooth surface. —*v.* To make wrinkles in: *Don't wrinkle the paper.*

write | rīt | *v.* **wrote** | rōt |, **writ•ten** | **rĭt′** n |, **writ•ing.** To form letters on a surface with a pen or pencil.

wrong | rông | *or* | rŏng | *adj.* **1.** Not correct: *a wrong answer.* **2.** Contrary to morality or law: *Lying is wrong.*

Y

yawn | yôn | *v.* To open the mouth wide and take in breath when sleepy.

yd yard.

yes•ter•day | **yĕs′** tər dā′ | *or* | -dē | *n.* The day before today.

you'd | yŏŏd |. You had.

yours | yŏŏrz | *or* | yôrz | *or* | yōrz | *pron.* Used to indicate that something belongs to you: *That book is yours.*

Z

ze•bra | **zē′** brə | *n.* An African animal related to the horse.

ze•ro | **zîr′** ō | *or* | **zē′** rō | *n., pl.* **ze•ros** or **ze•roes. 1.** The numerical symbol "0." **2.** The temperature on a scale indicated by this symbol.

zoo | zŏŏ | *n.* A park where animals are kept and shown.

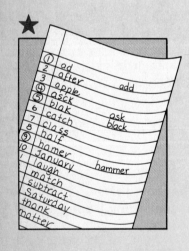

THE CHECKPOINT
Study Plan

When you have finished a Checkpoint page and you know that you have the correct answers, use the Checkpoint page and this Study Plan to test yourself.

★ Cover your answers to the Checkpoint page with a piece of paper. Number the paper 1 through 20. For each spelling clue, do steps 1, 2, and 3.

1 Read the clue and say the answer.

2 Spell the answer aloud.

3 Write the answer.

★ Uncover your first answers and do steps 4, 5, and 6.

4 Check your answers.

5 Circle the number of each misspelled word.

6 Write the correct spelling next to each incorrect word.

★ To study, cover your answers again, and fold the paper so that only the numbers show. For each circled number, repeat steps 1 through 6.